Table of Contents

BEDTIME STORIES FOR KIDS

Relaxing Meditation Sleep Stories for Every Night with Dinosaurs, Enchanted Creatures and Funny Animals

Olivia Bryce

INTRODUCTION

Lay comfortably in your bed. Close your eyes and imagine that you are lying on a soft blanket under the stars, with a gentle fire crackling nearby. You and your family are getting ready for bed, so you get comfortable and cozy on the blanket and prepare to listen to a soothing bedtime story.

You can hear waves crashing softly in the distance, and as you lay here, you feel as if you are surrounded by a warm, fluffy cloud. As the story begins, you let yourself relax and get carried away in the adventure. So, close your eyes and let the story begin...

Freya's Adventure with the Four-Legged Fairy

Freya was a little girl who lived in Saint Albert with her parents, her sister, and her dog, Shawty. Freya and her sister were always fighting, and this made their Mom unhappy.

Freya was seven years old while Freya's sister, Olivia, was four. Freya would refuse to give Olivia her toys to play with and would not pet Olivia when she was crying. Freya also could not allow Olivia to play with Shawty. Their parents were too poor to get Olivia new toys, or another dog, and Olivia would cry a lot.

'Freya, Olivia is your baby sister. Please share your things with her. Don't make her cry.' Their mother would often say, but Freya would not listen to her.

On Saturdays, Freya's father went to the stream to catch some fish. Freya always asked her father to take her along, but he would refuse and tell Freya that he wouldn't take her with him till she became a good sister to Olivia.

One day, Freya's Mom got back to the house with some good news; she had eventually gotten a part-time job. She would be leaving the house quite early every day so she could work her shift and come back by afternoon. The family was happy.

The following Saturday, Freya's father took his fishing line as usual and went to the stream. He told Freya to take care of her sister while he and their mum were away. Freya had always wanted to go with her dad, so she saw her opportunity that. As her father left, she also crept out of the house. Freya's father did not know that his daughter had followed him.

Freya tried to walk behind her father, so he would not see her. She did not take her dog with her because she feared that it would make some noise and give her away. Freya soon lost her father and lost her way. She tried going back to the house but discovered that she could not find her way back to the house. Then, she started to cry and cried till she fell asleep.

When she woke up a few hours later, she found herself in a strange forest; the trees were very short, and the leaves were not green in color but blue with white stripes. She screamed aloud, but it seemed nobody heard her voice because nobody answered her.

Freya became very hungry, and she looked around, but it seemed that there was nothing to eat. She kept walking till she got to a mango tree with ripe fruits. She threw some stones at the trees, and some of the fruits fell. She ate the mangoes happily.

When Freya became hungry again, she went back to the mango tree, but the mango tree had grown taller. Then it occurred to her that she was in a strange forest. She became afraid. She took some stones and threw them at the tree again, but no mango fell. Freya was sad.

She sat at the foot of the tree, and she thought she heard some voices. She got up to see where the noise was coming from, and she saw different animals in the distance; they were approaching the mango tree. Though the mango tree had grown taller, Freya summoned courage and climbed it. She did not want to be at the foot of the tree when the animals got there.

The animals gathered under the tree and had a meeting. Freya could not understand what they were saying, but she was glad that they did not see her where she was on top of the tree. She was tired and hungry, so she slept on the mango tree. She didn't wake up till the next day.

Freya woke up on the tree and looked around, there were no animals in the distance, but she could not see anybody too.

'Where are Mom and Dad? Why are they not out looking for me?

'I miss Olivia.' She said and started crying again. She wished she was good to Olivia. She wished she allowed her to play with her toys and with her dog. Maybe she wouldn't have left the house if she had been good to her sister.

'I am sorry for everything, Olivia. If I ever get back home, I promise to be a good sister to you.' She said out loud and closed her eyes.

Suddenly, she heard a voice behind her; the voice sounded like Olivia's. 'Did you call my name?' the voice asked. Freya turned only to see a fairy on four legs. The fairy was standing on one of the leaves of the tree.

'I didn't call your name.' Freya found it difficult to get the words out of her mouth.

'but I heard my name.' The fairy insisted, 'My name is Olivia.'

'Oh, my sister's name is Olivia, and I was referring to her.' Freya said.

Freya told the fairy how she had missed her way while trying to follow her father. She also told the fairy how she had always fought with her sister and had refused to allow her sister to play with her dog.

The fairy promised to go to Freya's house and inform her parents of where she was. Freya thanked her, and the fairy left.

When the fairy got to their house, it was in a mess. Freya's Mom had scattered everywhere because she could not find her daughter. Olivia was in the room crying because her sister was nowhere to be found. Shawty, the dog, was also barking uncontrollably. Freya's father was just returning from another trip to the cops.

The fairy went to Olivia in the room and stood in front of her. Olivia, who was crying, wiped her tears. She was surprised to see a fairy standing on four legs.

'Hello, Olivia. My name is Olivia.' The fairy said.

'Hello, fairy. I have never seen a fairy before. I only read about them in books. I am happy to see you, but I am also surprised that your name is Olivia, and you are walking on four legs.' Olivia replied.

'We will be friends from now on, but right now, we need to help Freya.' The fairy said.

When Olivia heard the fairy mention Freya, she jumped to her feet immediately. 'Have you found my sister? Do you know where she is?'

'Yes, I know where she is. Go and inform your father so I can take him to the forest now.'

Olivia rushed to inform her father, who also went to report to the cops so he could get some escort. Some men were told to go with him, and the fairy took them to where Freya was.

It was freezing, and Freya had almost passed out in the cold. Her father carried her and took her home.

Freya was sick for about five days, and everyone in the house took turns taking care of her. Even the fairy often dropped by to check on her.

When Freya got better, she apologized to her sister. 'I am sorry for everything, Olivia. I promise to be a good sister from today. We will play with Shawty together.' Freya hugged Olivia tightly.

This made everyone happy.

Ayana, the Proud Princess with a Heart of Beauty

A very long time ago, when man and animals lived together, there was a beautiful princess named Ayana. Ayana lived in a very big palace with her parents, the King and Queen of Salisha Kingdom. Ayana was the only child of her parents, and she was to become Queen after her father's death. She was beautiful and intelligent, but she was also wicked and lazy. She refused to help anyone who asked for her help, and she could not do any house chores. These kept young men from asking for her hand in marriage though she was grown enough to be married.

The King and Queen had often warned her about her wickedness and lazy attitude, but Ayana didn't listen to them.

'I am a Princess; I am also the future Queen. I don't need to be kind to anybody. I will always have subjects, so I will have many people to do the house chores, so I don't have to learn how to do them.' Ayana thought.

The Princess made her maids do all the house chores and would punish them if they didn't do it well. Her maids did not like her, but they kept serving her all the same.

Ayana was also proud. She refused to make friends with the people of Salisha Kingdom. She said she could only make friends with other princesses like her. She was the only princess in the kingdom. Other princesses lived far away in their kingdoms, so Ayana was often lonely. To kill boredom, she went to the forest every evening to read, meditate and have a stroll.

She was a princess and heiress to the throne. She hardly left the palace without her guards and some of her maids.

One evening, she went to the forest as usual. After her reading and meditation, she decided to take a stroll through the forest, and she saw a deer held in a trap.

'Help, help,' the deer cried out to Ayana.

'Are you talking to me? Do you know who I am? I am the Princess of the Salisha Kingdom and the future Queen. I am sorry, I can't get my hands dirty because I want to help you.' The Princess replied.

'Please, Princess, you don't have to get your hands dirty. You can ask one of your guards or maids to help me. I am in severe pain here.'

'I am sorry little deer; I can't help you. My maids and guards are paid to work for me and not you. You should be more careful next time, so you don't get stuck in a trap'. Ayana said and left with her maid and guards without helping the deer.

The little deer cried and cried, but Ayana didn't go back to help.

By nightfall, a fairy passed by the deer and heard his cry. The fairy helped the deer to remove the trap and checked his wound.

'Oh dear, the trap has cut you so deep. How long have you been here? Didn't anyone pass by?' The fairy asked the deer.

The fairy got some oil and poured it on the deer's wound so the deer could get better.

'Thanks, fairy. You have a kind heart. Princess Ayana of Salisha was here earlier. I pleaded and pleaded with her, but she didn't help me.' The deer told the fairy.

The fairy was not happy to hear that. 'I will help you get out of this forest, and I will go to Ayana immediately.'

'Please don't hurt her.' The deer pleaded.

'I won't.' The fairy promised. 'I just want to teach her a lesson or two.'

When the fairy got to Salisha Kingdom, the Princess was just about to sleep. The fairy saw as she ordered her maids around and made one of the maids stay up while she slept. Ayana always had a maid, and a guard stay awake while she slept.

The fairy flew in through the window and waved a magic wand. In an instant, Ayana became a maid while the maid became Ayana.

The fairy waited till Ayana woke up, then it told her what had happened. Ayana pleaded and pleaded that the fairy should reverse what it had done, but the fairy only flew out of the window. Ayana, the maid, remembered how the deer had pleaded with her the previous day that she should release it from a trap and how she had said no despite how he pleaded.

The maid, who was now the Princess, made Ayana do all the house chores and didn't allow the other maids to help her. This continued for three months, and Ayana this made Ayana change her ways. She not only became hardworking; she also became very humble and kind.

Sometimes later, the King of Salisha hosted a festival. The deer that the Princess met in the forest also came for the festival. When it saw the new Princess and the new maid, it knew that Ayana was the new maid and the person fronting as Princess was a maid. It knew that very well because it had seen both of them in the forest the other day.

The deer knew that it was the fairy at work. It went back into the forest to search for the fairy. The deer did not find the fairy till two months after that. The deer pleaded with the fairy to go back to Salisha kingdom and undo what it had done to Princess Ayana. The deer assured the fairy that the Princess had changed her ways.

One night, after a hard day's work, Ayana, the maid, became very tired, and she slept off. Then, the fairy came back with the magic wand. It waved it, and it undid what it had done before.

Ayana soon returned to the Princess she was, and the maid went back to being a maid.

Princess Ayana became very kind, and this made her parents very happy. A young and handsome prince from another kingdom also came and asked for her hand in marriage. Ayana said yes, and they lived happily ever after.

Lily and Rose's Fantastic Journey Through the Wilds

Lily and Rose were very good friends. Their parents lived close to one another, and both girls often visited each other's houses. Lily was six while Rose was five. They attended the same school, which was not very far from their houses. Both girls would go to school together in the morning and come back in the afternoons. They did not allow their parents to carry them in their cars because they wanted to enjoy their city's view.

They played together in school and played when they got home with Lily's dog.

One Monday morning, it was announced in school that the students would be going on a trip to the Wilds of Mona. All the children were happy to hear that, and they told their parents to pay for the trip. Lily and Rose were among the first students to pay. On the day of the trip, they got to school very early, and their teachers gave them some rules for the trip. They were always to stay together and scream if they noticed anything dangerous or were in danger.

When they got to the Wilds, the children were taken around by the guide. The children had a great time, and finally, it was time to go home. Lily looked around, but she could not find Rose, so she went back to look for her.

She found Rose sitting under a tree and playing with some butterflies.

'It's time to go home.' Lily announced.

'Rose, these butterflies are very beautiful. I wish I could take them with me.'

As Rose stretched her hand to catch the butterflies, they flew farther into the forest, and both girls went after them. The butterflies went farther and farther into the forest, and the girls kept following them. They eventually caught some, and they put them inside their bags.

Then, they tried going back to join the others. They went back through the path they thought they had come from but found themselves at the spot where they caught the butterflies. They decided to take another route, but they also found themselves in the same place.

Lily and Rose knew what had happened; they were lost!

Rose wanted to cry, but Lily told her not to.

'Don't cry, Rose. The teachers will soon know that we are missing and will come looking for us. Let us go round and enjoy the view of this forest before our teachers get here.'

Lily and Rose wandered through the forest, laughing, and singing as they went. They caught more butterflies and picked some fruits. As they kept walking through the forest, they saw a cave with a very small opening.

'We should go in,' Lily said.

'No, we should not. It might not be safe'. Rose replied.

'Well, you can stay outside, but I am going in.'

Lily went towards the mouth of the cave, and Rose followed her. They entered the cave but couldn't see a thing because it was very dark.

'Hello, is anyone here?' Lily called out.

Nobody answered, and she called out again.

Suddenly, the cave became very bright, as if someone had put a torch there. The girls were amazed. Then, they heard a loud growl behind them.

The girls were afraid, and they held on to each other. They turned and looked at what made the noise. They saw a big white horse with a very long horn.

'It's a Unicorn.' Rose whispered and held tightly to Lily.

The two girls tried going out of the cave, but they discovered that they could not find the opening through which they got in.

'What are you two doing here?' The Unicorn asked angrily.

'We lost our way,' the two girls stammered.

The Unicorn was angrier. 'You girls are not telling the truth. What brought you into my cave?'

'We are very sorry. We didn't know that it was your cave.' Lola answered.

The Unicorn moved towards them, and the girls became more afraid. Its footsteps sounded like mighty thuds on the floor of the cave.

'I will teach you two how not to trespass.' The Unicorn said and advanced towards the girls. They ran from one end of the cave to the other, but the Unicorn was faster than they were; it caught up with them and put both of them on its horn. It flung them many times in the air, and the girls begged it to stop, but it would not listen.

Then, the Unicorn put the girls down and blew air from its mouth towards them. The girls immediately drifted into a deep sleep. They slept and slept for many days.

When they woke up, the Unicorn was nowhere to be found.

'Let's get out of here before the Unicorn gets back.' Rose said, and they got up quickly. They went around the cave, but there was no opening for them to get out. Suddenly, they heard footsteps that sounded like those of the Unicorn in the distance.

They went back to the spot where they were before and pretended to be asleep.

'Get up, you girls. I know that you are not sleeping. I will release you, girls, now, but you must never do this again. It is not safe for children to roam the forest alone. They could get killed. Your parents and teachers are worried sick about you. You should not take them through this trouble again.'

The two girls were very happy. They got up and thanked the Unicorn and asked for the way out of the cave. The Unicorn went towards the wall of the cave and tapped it with its horn. Suddenly, there was an opening in the wall, and the girls left the cave.

They had not eaten for days, and this made them very tired.

Lily and Rose held hands and kept walking, not knowing where they were going.

They kept walking till both girls fainted in the forest. A familiar noise woke them up, the barking of Lily's dog.

The police had taken the dog with them in their search for the girls. The two girls were taken to their parents, who were very happy to see them.

'We are sorry, Mom and Dad. We won't do that again.' Both girls said at the same time.

Their parents hugged them, 'It is okay, girls. We are glad that you both are safe now. Let us get you two to a hospital.'

Spooky, the Friendly Feathered Hero!

Once upon a time in the Birds' Kingdom, there was a very big mahogany tree where all the birds nested. There were different kinds of birds, and they all lived as one big happy family.

The most beautiful of all the birds was a bird named Spooky. She had beautiful feathers and a lovely beak. Spooky used its feathers to keep warm and stay healthy. She also used her beak to catch worms for herself and other animals who could not go out to hunt.

Spooky was also a kind bird, and all the birds agreed to make her Queen.

The birds often gather to hold meetings on matters that affected all of them, and one day, they gathered to discuss their carnival. The carnival is held once every year, and the most interesting part of it was the beauty contest where three beautiful birds would be chosen. All the birds kept their feathers clean and oily for that special day.

The birds would also prepare a lot to eat and drink and go to other animal kingdoms and invite them for the event.

Though Spooky came first every year, other birds still competed for second and third positions. The carnival lasted five days, and it was a period of merriment for the birds.

While they were preparing for the next carnival, a little bird flew to the tree. They knew that the bird was not a part of their kingdom because they could identify everyone in their kingdom. It was a stray bird that had lost her way. The bird was dirty and smelly, and all the other birds stayed away from her. The bird was also shivering because she had lost most of her feathers.

'Help, help,' the bird cried.

'My father went out to hunt, and I was alone with my mother. My mother slept off, and a great hawk took her away before I could wake her. I only managed to escape from the hawk. I have been looking for my father for a very long time. I didn't find him and also lost my way home. Please help me.'

'Why did your family decide to stay alone? Why didn't they join us here? Our hawks do not prey on smaller birds.' Some of the birds said, refusing to help the small bird.

Then Spooky spoke up, 'What is your name, little bird?'

'My name is Bubba.' The little bird replied.

Spooky told Bubba that she was going to give her some of her feathers. 'I will give you some of my colorful feathers so you can also be as beautiful as I am.'

The other birds told Spooky not to give out her feathers. Some of them told her that she would lose the competition if she did; some even told her that she might die if she gave out some of her feathers.

Spooky did not listen to the other birds; instead, she told them that it was good to be kind and help others because we might also need help in the future. She gave the little bird some feathers, and the little bird also became beautiful.

Spooky asked Bubba if she would like to join their kingdom, but the little bird politely refused. 'Many thanks for your feathers, Spooky, but I am sorry I won't be able to join this kingdom. I want to go out to look for my father. The hawk might have killed my mother, but I am sure that my father is out there, maybe in danger and in need of help. I am sorry I must go. I will always remember your kind act. Thank you, Spooky. I am grateful.'

'It is okay, Bubba. You really don't have to stay here. You should go and find your father, but you should be very careful out there.' Spooky told the bird.

Then, the little bird left the mahogany tree in search of her father.

The Bird's Kingdom's carnival was held that year, but Spooky did not win first place for the Most Beautiful Bird. Another bird did. Spooky was not discouraged. She told herself that she was going to groom her feathers so she could win the competition the following year.

Some years later, Spooky fell ill, and she began to lose some of her fine feathers. The bird's doctor tried to nurse her back to health, but he could not really do much because Spooky's feathers were just falling off. The other birds tried giving Spooky some feathers because they did not want her to die, but the doctor told them that their feathers might not suit Spooky. Only her feathers could work for her.

That was when one of them remembered the little bird that Spooky gave some feathers to so many years ago. They put together a team to go and search for that bird to see if they could get some feathers from her to keep Spooky from dying. The team flew over many rivers and valleys, and the search went on for about two months. Finally, they found the bird on an island. The little bird was now big. It was also more beautiful than it had been the last time they saw it. There was a bigger bird close to it.

'Hello, Bubba. How are you doing? Do you still remember us?' The birds asked.

The bird did not reply to them. It only flew away.

The other birds tried flying after it, but they did not catch up with it.

Then, they went back to the second bird they found with the little bird on the island.

'Good day, sir. Please, we need Bubba's help. She did not even wait to hear us out before she flew away.'

Are you the birds from the kingdom?' the bigger bird asked. 'My daughter has told me a lot about your unkind attitude and how you almost convinced Spooky not to give her any feathers. If Spooky had not given her those feathers that day, she would have died, and I would have died too because she came to rescue me after she got the feathers from Spooky.'

The birds pleaded with Bubba's father and apologized for their behavior. They also told him their mission. Bubba's father promised to talk to his daughter.

The birds left him and went back to their kingdom.

Bubba got back to her father later in the evening, and her father told her what had happened. She flew to the Mahogany tree immediately.

When she got there, she saw that Spooky was not in good shape. About four birds had to stay close to her to keep her warm. Bubba gave Spooky some feathers, and the doctor applied an ointment. He also gave her some herbs. Bubba stayed on the Mahogany tree till Spooky got better.

Spooky thanked Bubba for saving her life, and Bubba also thanked Spooky for helping her many years ago.

'It is good to be good.' The doctor who had been listening to both said.

Ben's Purr-fectly Fun Friendship with a Talking Cat

Ben was the only child of his parents. His parents were often busy, and Ben was usually very lonely.

He was a sickly child and went to the hospital often. His parents did not allow him to go to school because of his health. They got him a home teacher who came to the house to teach him to read and write. Ben also had a nanny who stayed with him while his parents were at work.

Ben's parents got him a lot of toys and videos so he could not be lonely, but Ben was not happy because he could not play with other children. He wanted to attend a regular school just like them.

One day, when Ben was coming back from the hospital, he spotted a lone cat that looked unhappy. Ben thought he could see himself in the cat, so he asked his Mom to stop by so they could help the cat.

They parked the car and went to the cat. The cat was unwell; they took it to the car and took it straight to a doctor. The cat was with the doctor for some days, after which she was given back to Ben.

'Don't worry, fluffy one. I will take you to my house, and you will not be out alone anymore. I will always be your friend.' Ben told the cat.

Ben took the cat to his house and gave her some milk. The cat finished the milk in no time and went to sleep.

Ben woke up severally in the middle of the night to check on the cat.

He wanted to make sure that the cat was okay.

The next day, Ben went to the study to do the homework that his home teacher had given him the previous day. The cat came in and sat opposite Ben quietly.

'Hello, Kathie. How are you doing today?' Ben spoke to the cat. He had given the cat a name, Kathie.

The cat gave no reply. It only wagged its tail and went back inside.

The next day, Ben went to study, and the cat came in again. The cat snuggled close to Ben and spoke. 'Hello, Ben.'

Ben was surprised to see a cat talking.

The cat continued, 'Don't be scared, Ben. I got lost when I went out to play with my friends. And that was where you found me. I am sure that my Mom would be out looking for me now. Please can you take me back to my mother? We live with the Simpsons on Thailand Avenue. I don't know how to get there, but I am sure that you can ask your dad or Mom to help. Please, you have to hurry, the Simpsons want to move house.'

Though Ben did not want Kathie to leave him, he promised to help her all the same. He told his parents about it, and his Mom drove Ben and the cat down to Thailand Avenue.

They got to the Simpsons' address, but a neighbor told them that the Simpsons relocated the previous day, and he did not know their new address.

Kathie's eyes fell.

'What do you want to do now?' Ben asked Kathie.

'Please take me back with you. I have found a new family in your house."

Ben was happy. He put Kathie back in the car, and they all went back to the house.

Ben was no longer lonely because he could now play with Kathie. Ben's health also started to improve. He got better every day.

The Amazing Adventures of Brave Queen Jenny

A very long time ago, there was a quiet village called Amata Village. It was at the end of many oceans and seas. The villagers were very quiet and peaceful, but they could not leave their village. A fearsome monster kept them from going out of their village and interacting with people from other villages. The monster lived on the outskirts of the village.

The monster would also go to their farms at night and steal their crops and farm animals. No trap could catch him, and no one who went to fight him ever came back to tell the story, which kept the villagers in constant fear. The weapons in their armory soon got dusty because no one was willing to use them.

The monster kept tormenting the people, and it seemed there was nothing they could do about it. They did not have an internal army that could fight him, and they also could not seek external help.

The King had two children: Prince Jerry, who was fifteen years old, and Princess Jenny, who was just twelve. According to tradition, either of them could sit on the throne after the demise of their father, so they were sometimes allowed to sit with their father during his meetings with the chiefs or the villagers.

Jenny was intelligent. She loved to read, and one would find her reading when she had nothing to attend to. She read a lot of books and had knowledge of several topics that some of her teachers didn't. She often heard the villagers talk about a certain monster who had been oppressing them for about ten years. It seemed the villagers were at their wit's end, and it was sadder because her father did not know what to do. Jenny became concerned. She wanted to help the villagers but how could she? She had read of different women heroes in history and felt she would be one of them. She wondered what a little girl like she might had to possess to overpower the monster. 'All things are possible for me, only if I will believe.' She said to herself one day after hours of being in thought. Suddenly, an idea flashed through her mind, and she jumped up happily, 'I can do it, I can do it.' She said and danced around the room.

One of her maids came in. 'Princess Jenny, I hope you are fine? Why are you not sleeping? It is late already. Is there anything I can help you with?'

'Don't worry. I am fine. You can go back to your room now.' Jenny said and dismissed the maid.

Jenny asked the elders who knew about the monster to tell her about him. She wanted to know all about the monster so she could plan her strategy.

An old man was the only one who ever went to the monster and came back alive. The old man told Jenny that the monster kept all his prisoners in a large well at night, and he made them work his farm and do other chores from morning till evening. He often beat them and did not give them good food. He showed no mercy to the weak or sick, and he would beat them till they got back to work.

Jenny knew she could not fight the monster alone; she needed help. She wondered who would be brave enough to face the monster with her. She also wanted to keep it a secret; the villagers should be unaware of her plans till the day they would leave for the monster's house.

She thought of an unlikely group of people; young and fearless girls like her. They would come together and plan on how to take the monster down.

She started to talk to her friends secretly about her plans.

Soon enough, Princess Jenny started an army of young girls.

Every night, the girls met in a hidden chamber in the palace, and Jenny taught them how to fight. She had learned from the different books she had read, and she gladly shared her knowledge with the girls. They trained for hours every night, and after about six months, Jenny felt they were ready for the fight. She got some weapons from the kingdom's armory and oiled and cleaned them. Then, she announced her plans to her father.

Her father called a meeting of the chiefs and the girls' parents, and he told them about the mission of the girls. Though their parents were concerned for their safety, they prayed that they would all come back safely.

Finally, it was time for the girls to set out; they marched on to the outskirts of the village and sang as they went.

We are the girls of Amata
We are fearless
We are brave
We will protect our fathers
We will fight for our mothers
We will watch no ill befall our siblings
We will defeat the monster
We are afraid of him no more

The villagers watched them with mixed feelings; they were happy that the girls were taking it up to fight for the village, but they also feared for the safety of the girls.

The King promised to give each girl a bag of gold if they came back safely. He also promised to give a half bag of gold to their families.

The girls got to the outskirts of the village by nightfall, and good enough for them; the monster was sleeping. He had no idea that some people were coming to fight him, so he was not prepared. There was a hole in which the monster lived. An adult could not easily go through, and that was the monster's leverage. He would cleverly come out while an intruder was trying to come in, tie up the intruder, and cast a spell on him. The spell kept them from ever trying to find their way back home. They then became slaves and prisoners to the monster.

Jenny and her girls were kids, so they easily slid into the hole while the monster was still asleep.

Though the monster was not prepared for a fight, he got up immediately after one of the girls got close to him. He was about to hit the girl when Jenny came from behind and hit his hand with a sword. His hand went limp. In the same instant, Jenny hit one of his legs, and the monster was down on his knees. The other girls came closer and dealt many blows to the monster till he passed out.

They searched his house and found an elixir for his spell.

The girls tied up the monster securely and rushed to the dry well where they found the prisoners, just like the old man had told Jenny. Jenny released all the prisoners and gave them the elixir to cure the spell cast on them by the monsters. They were all very happy, and they thanked the girls for their bravery. Jenny threw the monster into the well, then placed a secured covering over it. She then counted all her girls. None of them had died in the fight, though some of them were severely wounded.

Jenny had some salve with her, which she applied to their wounds. The strong girls assisted in carrying the weak ones, and they all marched to town with the prisoners. As they got closer to the village, they sang the song they had sung on their way out, this time with a little twist.

We are the girls of Amata
We are fearless
We are brave
We will protect our fathers
We will fight for our mothers
We will watch no ill befall our siblings
We have defeated the monster
We will no longer be afraid of him

The villagers did not sleep through the night. They spent all night in prayers that the girls would return safely and that their mission would be successful. The girls and prisoners got back to the village the next day, and as soon as the villagers heard their voices, they ran towards them, chanting victorious songs. It was a moment of reunion between long-lost family members.

The kingmakers had a meeting, and they agreed to make Jenny the next Queen after her father's demise. They were afraid that it might not go down well with Jerry, so they invited him for their discussion.

To their surprise, Jenny's brother, Jerry, did not object. 'My sister is a brave girl. The people of Amata Village deserve a leader like her.' He said.

They all applauded him as the Chief of the Kingmakers gave Jenny the 'next Queen's crown,' which she was to wear till she became Queen.

Happy Lucy

There was a young girl named Lucy. She was just four years old. Lucy and her mom had just moved to a new house. Lucy liked the old house better because she had many friends, and she was never lonely. There were no neighbors at the new house, and Lucy often felt lonely when her mom was not home.

One day, her mother told her that she would be traveling for a week.

'Who will take care of me while you are gone, mom?' Lucy asked her mother.

'Your aunt, Aunt Shirley, will come over and stay with you. I spoke with her already.'

'I don't know Aunt Shirley, mom. Please take me with you.' Lucy pleaded.

Lucy's mom told her that she could not take Lucy with her. She promised that her aunt would come over and Lucy would enjoy spending time with her.

The next day, Aunt Shirley came over, and Lucy's mom traveled.

When Lucy's aunt saw that Lucy's mother was gone, she also left the house and left Lucy to take care of herself.

Lucy became very sad. They had no neighbors, and there was no one to play with. She went to her room and cried. Lucy did not like being alone. When she was tired of crying, she went around the house to see if there was anything that she could do to pass the time. There was nothing to do, so she went outside and went to the back of the house. She saw a small gate which she opened and went in.

Lucy found herself in a very beautiful garden. Birds perched and sang as they moved from one tree to the other. The soil was so spongey and rich, and Lucy bent to scoop some with her hands. There were different flowers and herbs, and they all seemed to complement the fruits and vegetables. There was a gentle breeze, and the trees seemed to be dancing in tune with the breeze. Lucy closed her eyes and raised her head; she wanted to feel the breeze better. She also swayed her body in rhythm with the breeze. When she opened her eyes, she saw a rainbow in the sky.

There was a stream in the garden, and as Lucy got closer to it, she saw some gold and silver fishes! She reached out, brought some of them out, and put them back. The fish were not slimy, so she could hold them with her bare hands.

The scent from the hibiscus flowers was exotic. Lucy went closer to the flower, closed her eyes, and inhaled deeply. The scent seemed to clear away all her fears.

It was a beautiful sight indeed!

There were some butterflies on the flowers, and they were singing. Lucy listened carefully so she could learn the song and sing with them.

Beautiful butterflies are we
We are without a care in the world
We will remain beautiful
And that against all odds
Then, they sang another song.
Learn to be happy
Happiness is free
Learn to find it
And then be happy.

Lucy told herself that she was not going to worry anymore about her aunt. She was going to be happy all the same, even if there was someone to play with or not.

There was an orange tree in the garden, and Lucy saw that some of its fruits had fallen. She took one, peeled it, and took a bite. It was very sweet. Then, she ate two more oranges.

'I will keep some for Momma and Aunt Shirley.' She said and picked some more.

By noon, the garden had become hot because of the heat of the sun.

Lucy went back inside the house and put the oranges in the fridge. She brought out her box of colors. She drew and painted a picture of the garden she had just found; then she hung the picture in her room.

She also painted another picture and kept it in her room. She was going to give them to her mother when she was back.

Later in the evening, Aunt Shirley got back and made dinner. She served Lucy some food and went straight to bed.

Lucy also went to bed dreaming about the garden.

Aunty Shirley woke up very early the next day and made breakfast for herself and Lucy. Then, she took her bag and was about to leave the house when Lucy ran after her, 'I have some oranges for you, Aunty.'

"Thanks, dear. I'll get them when I'm back. I am late for a meeting.' Aunty Shirley said and left.

After she left, Lucy took her breakfast and went to the garden.

That was what Lucy did every day while her mom and aunt were away; she spent time in the garden and later went to draw. She was no longer unhappy.

One day, as Lucy left the garden and went to draw, she heard the horn of her mom's car. She ran outside immediately and gave her mum a big hug.

'Welcome Mommy, I have missed you.' Lucy said.

'I have missed you too, my baby.' Lucy's mum replied.

Lucy's mother had bought some gifts for her daughter, and she brought them out of the car and gave them to her. Lucy's eyes light with glee. 'Thank you, Mommy.'

Later that night, as Lucy's mother tucked her in bed, she told her how her aunt would always leave her at home whenever her mom was not around.

'I'm sorry, my Princess. Lucy's mother apologized. I will find more time to be with you as from now.'

Lucy smiled, closed her eyes, and inhaled deeply. I love you, Mommy, and you know what, Mommy? I will tell you about the beautiful garden I found tomorrow. I have painted many pictures of it already so we can hang it in all the rooms in the house, but I need you to see the garden.'

I love you too, Princess. It's okay. I can't wait to hear about it.

Lucy's mom gave her a peck on the forehead, and Lucy drifted into a beautiful sleep.

The Shadowland Adventure of the Braxton Kids

The Braxton kids were four boys who lived beside my grandfather's house. Grandfather did not allow me to play with them because grandpa said they were bad boys.

'I don't want you to learn their ways,' my grandfather would often say to me.

The Braxton kids were quintuplets; they were all born the same day. They were also identical, and their mom made them wear bracelets with their names on them so they could be easily recognized. Some people call them quins, which was short for quintuplets. They lived in a very big house that had many rooms. They had many servants that did all the house chores, and this made the Braxton kids very lazy. They were also unkind to their servants.

Though there were many rooms in their house, their mother gave the four of them one very big room. She wanted them always to stay together so they could bond as brothers.

After one year of staying together in one room and fighting every day, the Braxton kids eventually moved to separate rooms in the house.

Their mother became very sad. One day, she was sulking about the behavior of her children when her father came in.

'Why are you sad, Ronnie?' Her father asked.

'My children never seem to agree on anything. They are always fighting about everything. They also lie, and they steal and cheat.'

'Don't worry, my daughter. They are only kids. They will soon outgrow this bad behavior.' Grandpa tried to reassure Ronnie.

Ronnie screamed, 'They will be ten years old in two months, Dad. When will they stop fighting one another?'

Their wise old grandfather told their mother to allow them to visit the land of the shadows for a few days. He assured her that they would come back changed boys.

Their mother disagreed at first. She was scared for her sons' safety, but she gave in after grandfather assured her, he would speak to the Shadow-King before the boys would go and no harm would befall the boys.

Grandfather called the boys and told them that they would be visiting the land of the shadows. He asked them if they would like to go together, but they all chorused No. Each boy wanted to go alone.

So, Grandpa told them that they would not go together; each boy would come back before the other could go. Each boy would spend five days over there and come back. They were also not allowed to tell one another of their experiences till they had all gone and come back. The boys had mixed feelings; they did not know what to expect as they had never heard of any place called the land of the shadows before then and didn't know what to expect but were happy that they would not be going with their siblings. They didn't like one another anyway.

Jason's Adventure

Jason was the first of the quins to go to the land of the shadows. It was dark when he got there, and he was hungry. He walked around trying to find someone to talk to or something to eat but didn't see anyone. He saw a small hut and walked in.

He saw a plate of food on a table, and he called out, but nobody answered him. He ate the food and wiped his mouth clean. He was happy that he didn't go with his brothers, so there was no one to share the food with. He went out and saw another hut, he went in and called out again, and still, nobody answered. He saw a bed with his name on it. He also saw some clothes on the bed. He was sure that that was the hut prepared for him because grandfather had told him that necessary arrangements had been made in advance for his arrival.

The next day, he took his bath and changed into clean clothes, and he took a walk around the town. He didn't see anyone, but this time, he heard voices. He was afraid, and he hurried back to the hut that had a bed with his name on it. When he got to the hut, he saw that someone had been there, and the person had left a note. 'Be at the town square by 3.' He wondered who came in while he was outside.

By 3 pm, he got to the town square, and he saw shadows. There were so many of them, and the shadows were talking. One of them asked him who ate the food at the royal table the previous night. Jason denied eating it. They told him that his shadow was with him while he was eating, and shadows never lie. Jason then confessed to eating the food.

They told him that his punishment would be to clear the weeds at the royal farm throughout his stay. He would only be given food and water once a day, and if he misbehaved, there would be another punishment.

Jason was taken to the farmland, and he burst into tears. It was a vast expanse of land.

'If my brothers were here, they would have helped me with this. I promise to be a good boy as from now on.'

By the last day of Jason's visit, he was almost through with clearing the farmland, and he was allowed to go back home.

Julian's Adventure

When Jason got back to the house, it was Julian's turn to go. Julian wanted to ask Jason about his experience secretly, but he thought Jason might not be willing to tell him anything since they were not on talking terms. It was also against the rules anyway, so he decided against it. He was going to go without anyone telling him anything in advance, and he was going to come back with his stories.

He said goodbye to his mom and left. He got there by midday when the Shadows were having lunch at the town square. They invited him over and gave him a very big bowl of food. Julian was happy that he wouldn't be sharing the food with anyone, so he sat down and happily devoured the food.

The Shadow-King then gave him some instructions; Julian would be staying at a big house throughout his stay, but he could only enter his room. He must not enter the other rooms in the house. The Shadows wouldn't always be around, so he had to take care of himself. However, they would make sure that he was safe and had enough to eat. He was to return to the town square the next day by 10 am.

When Julian got to the house, he was happy that he would be staying in such a fine house but was disappointed when he got to his room. His room looked so dirty and unkempt. There was a broom and a mop stick, and water was running, but Julian was not used to cleaning, so he left the cleaning items where he met them.

He told himself that he wouldn't sleep in that messy room but would get a clean room to sleep in. They won't know if I enter another room. Julian said to himself. He went to where the room keys were kept and brought out some keys. Julian started trying them on the doors one after the other. He saw that all the other rooms were clean except for his. He decided to sleep on the one with the biggest bed.

The next day, he woke up very early, took his bath, locked up the room, and returned the key. When it was almost 10, he left for the village square. The Shadow-King asked him if he enjoyed his sleep, and he said yes. He further asked him how he enjoyed sleeping in such a dirty room. Julian told him that he had cleaned the room before he slept.

The Shadow-King told Julian that his shadow slept in another room throughout the night, and there was no record of his shadow cleaning any of the rooms. In fact, Julian's shadow visited all the rooms before he slept.

Julian was ashamed of himself, and he could not deny any of the accusations.

The Shadow-King announced his punishment. He would clean the room he was given every day and sweep the town square for four days.

Julian had no one to help him, and he did his chores all alone.

On the fifth day, he was allowed to go home. He made a promise before leaving the land of the shadows that he would turn a new leaf.

Jayden's Adventure

Jayden was not very happy about going to the land of the shadows. Though Jason and Julian did not tell him about their experiences there, he had seen the look on their faces when they got back. He was scared, but grandfather told him that he had to go all the same.

The Shadows had already gathered by the time Jayden got there. They welcomed him and gave him some food and some drinks. The food and drinks were quite a lot, and Jayden was happy that he wouldn't share them with anyone. He sat down and ate, but he could not finish the food. He opened his bag and put the leftovers inside.

The Shadow-King told him that he had to be of good behavior and must not take or touch whatever does not belong to him. The King further told him that arrangements had been made for his stay and he need not worry about anything. He only needed to walk around the town to find what had been prepared for his arrival. Then, the Shadow-King and the rest of the shadows disappeared.

Jayden walked around, and he saw two huts. One of them had his name on it; he went inside and saw a mat and a pillow. He wondered how he was going to sleep on the mat. He had never slept on a mat before. Then, it occurred to him that there might be a better place to spend the night, so he decided to take a stroll around the town.

The huts he saw were not much different from his, and he was about to give up and go back to his hut when he saw a building at the far end of the town. He kept walking and walking till he got to the building. Then, he entered and went from one room to the other.

When he got to the kitchen, he saw some eggs in a silver bowl. The eggs were unlike any he had ever seen; they were blue! Jayden wondered what the color of their yolks would be. He took one to get a closer look but downwards, the egg fell in his hand!

In a bid to leave the house in a hurry, his right leg hit a bucket on the door and the bucket also broke. Jayden was afraid, and he fled to his hut.

When he woke up the next morning, he took his bath and sat down. No one had brought food yet.

He opened his bag and saw that the leftovers he had kept there the previous day had already gone bad and could not be eaten. He went out to throw it away, then he saw a note by his door.

'Be at the town square by 10.'

Jayden knew that his secret had been discovered, but he wondered how that was because nobody saw him when he entered or left the house.

When he got to the town square, he was told that some items were broken at the palace the previous night. Jayden denied leaving his hut the previous night. Then, the Shadow-King showed him a picture of his shadow moving around the house and breaking some stuff. Jayden later admitted to breaking the items.

The Shadow-King told him that he wouldn't be punished for breaking those items but for lying. He was to assist the ladies in the kitchen in making food for the next four days. He was also to wash all the plates used by everyone.

Jayden wondered how a little lie could result in such punishment. He wished he had someone to help him with the chores.

The next day, while washing the plates, he became so tired that he went to sit under a tree.

'I miss my brothers.' Jayden sobbed.

When Jayden started crying, one of the shadows came to him. 'You should not cry. Don't worry. I will help you. Just make sure to turn a new leaf when you leave here.'

'Thanks, Shadow. I will remember your advice.'

The five days were soon over, and Jayden went back home.

Justin's Adventure

Justin was quite eager to go to the land of the shadows. He was the most adventurous of the four, and he had been counting days since the first day that Jason had left.

When he got there, he was given a grand welcome. They also told him to be of his best behavior as any misconduct would attract punishment. He was shown to his hut, and then the Shadows left. They told him that they would be back the next day.

Justine looked around the hut; it was dusty and needed a lot of cleaning. Though there were some cleaning materials in the hut, Justin was not used to house cleaning, so he left the hut and took a walk around the town.

At the end of one of the roads, there was a beautiful house, and Justin walked in. The house had all sorts of fanciful household items.

I can't sleep in that small hut,' Justin said to himself. 'I will come back here at nightfall and sleep in this beautiful house.'

Later in the evening, Justin went to the beautiful house and slept on the grand bed. He woke up very early the next day and went to his hut. He was surprised to see a note by the door of his hut. 'Be at the town square by noon.'

He wondered who had kept the note there. He also wondered if the person knew that he didn't sleep at his hut over the night. He had his bath and got dressed for the meeting. He got to the town square by noon, and by then, the Shadows had already gathered.

Justin was accused of sleeping on the royal bed instead of sleeping on his bed. Justin asked how they had known, and they told him that his Shadow had given him away.

Your shadow is always with you. So, you should be mindful of your actions even when nobody is watching you. ' The Shadow-King told him.

Justin's punishment was announced: he would sweep and mop all the rooms in the King's house before he would be allowed to go back home.

It was pretty tasking, and Justin's back hurt often.

'I will stop all bad behavior from now on. I will also live in peace with my brothers.' He said to himself.

On the fourth day of his visit, there was still so much work to be done that he wondered if he would be allowed to go home the next day without finishing the chores.

When he got there on the last day of his visit, he saw that the work was almost completed. It was like someone had helped him with some of the work while he went to bed the last night. He praised himself for his perseverance and promised himself to be hardworking from then. He was also grateful to whoever had helped. He picked up a mop stick and continued the work. He was done before noon.

Then, the Shadows showed him the way home.

THE END

When Justin got back, grandpa allowed them to all relive their experiences. They all had stories to tell, and they learned some lessons from one another's experiences.

The Braxton kids all changed for good afterward. They became more loving and kinder, and hardworking. They also stopped lying and stealing, and this made their mother very happy.

They all moved back to the big room that their mom had prepared for them before.

On their next birthday, the Braxton kids decided to wear the same color of shirts and shorts. They all agreed that Jason would be the one to choose a color, and they would all go with his choice. Jason chose blue, and their mom bought them colorful blue shirts and shorts. They had a blue-themed birthday party which was all fun.

42

The Dreaming Dino Discovery

A very long time ago, Dinosaurs only lived on trees; they hopped from one tree to another, just like monkeys. They often live together in very big trees. Dinosaurs didn't wake up late; they loved to wake up early so they could go out and hunt for the day. The big dinosaurs would go out early and hunt for food while the young ones would stay back on the tree.

Dina, the dinosaur, didn't like waking up early. She was a big dinosaur, but she often slept late, and so she would wake up late. Her father had often warned her about the dangers of waking up late. He told her that she might wake up so late that she wouldn't be able to get anything to eat that day.

Dina was often late for hunting, but she always came back with food to eat and also to share with the others. Other dinosaurs also warned Dina about her lateness in waking up, but Dina ignored all warnings.

One night, Dina slept late as usual, and there was heavy rainfall. Dina was still sleeping while the other dinosaurs went hunting. They didn't get much food that day because of the rain, so they got back early and shared the food they had brought.

Dina did not come back till later at night, she had hopped from tree to tree, but she had caught nothing. She asked the others to share some of their food with her, but everything had finished before she got back. She went to bed hungry.

That night, Dina went to bed early. She woke up early the next day so she could go hunting with the others.

The Curious Tale of the Winged Hen's Mystery

Brian and Houston will be going to Disneyland tomorrow. They are so excited, and they don't want to sleep. Momma takes them to their bedroom, and the boys take a shower. Then she tucks them in bed, and they ask her to tell them a story.

'Please tell us a story, Momma. We want to hear a story.'

Momma picks up a storybook and says to the boys. 'I will tell you a story about the hen.'

'Thanks, Momma. We want to hear about the hen.' The two boys say happily.

'A very long time ago, the hen could fly just like the other birds. She could also talk to humans and understood whatever Man said.

The hen and Man were very good friends, and they would often be seen together. Then, there was nothing such as a chicken meal because Man could not eat his friend.

One day, Man told the hen that he was going on a long journey, and he asked the hen to watch his house while he was away.

'We are friends. I will gladly watch your house till you are back.' The hen replied.

Man thanked the hen and left for the trip, and he came back in a couple of months. He had brought some gifts for the hen, and he went straight to the hen's house. Both of them were happy to see each other, and Man thanked the hen for watching his house while he was away.

When Man got to his house, he saw that some of his jewelry was missing. He called the hen and informed him, but the hen denied seeing any jewelry. He had to report to the local council.

The council summoned Man's neighbors and questioned them. Then, they invited the hen too. They all denied stealing the jewelry.

Man insisted that the hen had stolen the jewelry as he had asked the hen to take care of his house while he was away.

'Okay, if you find any of the stolen items with me, you can cut off my wings, and human beings can kill and eat me just like other animals.' The hen said and left the venue of the meeting angrily.

The search for the stolen items began, and all the houses were searched, but the items could not be found. The pig suggested that they search all the farmlands too. They searched the farmlands and saw the items on the hen's farmland. The hen was arrested, and he later confessed to stealing the jewelry.

The King ordered that the wings of the hen be trimmed. He also allowed human beings to kill and eat chicken, and that's why we had chicken and dumplings for lunch yesterday.

Mama finishes reading and sees that both boys are already sleeping. She closes the book and tiptoes to her room.

Meet the Splashing Water Dinosaur

Nathan loved dinosaurs, and Nathan would go through his collection of toys every night before he went to bed. This night was no different. Nathan hugged his favorite dinosaur to his chest. Pete was Nathan's favorite dinosaur because of its color. Nathan's favorite color was blue, and the stuffed dinosaur was also blue.

Nathan's mother and father walked in, and Nathan smiled at them. They came to Nathan every night to read him bedtime stories and tell him goodnight. Nathan was five years old, but he thought of himself as a baby since he was the only child in the house.

'Mama, papa,' Nathan called his parents, 'I want to go to the lake tomorrow.' The lake was where they usually go-to for picnics, and it was Nathan's favorite place.

'But you have school tomorrow,' Nathan's mother said.

'I don't want to go,' Nathan wailed. Nathan knew that if he cried, his parents would allow him to do whatever he wanted.

'Okay, we will go tomorrow," Nathan's mother said. She looked at his father, and he nodded.

'It is whatever you want, baby,' they both said. Nathan rejoiced to himself and smiled. He would take his dinosaurs to the lake the next day, and he would have so much fun playing with them and letting them swim in the water. Nathan's mother never worried about him dropping the plastic toys in the water. It was only the stuffed ones that he couldn't put in the water.

Nathan's mother and father read him a dinosaur story, and Nathan felt happy as they kissed him and left his room. The room was dark, but Nathan wasn't scared. He knew tomorrow would soon arrive, and he would have so much fun at the lake. Nathan fell asleep with the thoughts of the next day on his mind.

They were at the lake, and Nathan jumped. He was pleased. Being at the lake was better than being at school. His mother and father sat under a tree, eating apples. Nathan went to the lake and sat down beside the water. He placed his dinosaur toys beside him and put his feet in the water. The water was calm, and Nathan liked it. As the breeze blew and the water glittered in the sun, Nathan took his plastic dinosaurs and put them in the water. As he moved them in the cool water and laughed, he saw something in the water and stared. Nathan removed his toys from the water and put his hand inside to touch what he had seen. It was a purple dinosaur, and it came out of the water. It was beautiful, and it was bigger than Nathan. Nathan liked dinosaurs, but he had never seen a real one. He wanted to touch the dinosaur, but it looked angry.

'Why are you not in school?' the dinosaur asked him.

'Mama and Papa wanted to come to the lake,' Nathan lied.

'You are such a liar!' the dinosaur said. 'I don't like little liars like you.'

Nathan started crying. He wanted the dinosaur to like him.

'Why are you not in school?' the dinosaur asked again.

'I did not want to go,' Nathan said. He was still crying, and his eyes were red. His parents were on the other side, and they did not know what was happening.

'You are such a spoilt brat. Every child should be in school. You can come to the lake on Saturdays, not on school days. I don't like you.'

Nathan's lips shook. He was so sad and scared. Mama and papa had never called him a spoilt brat. They did the things he wanted, and he was always happy.

'Please, like me,' Nathan begged the dinosaur.

'Only if you change,' the dinosaur said.

'I will,' Nathan pleaded.

Nathan woke up. It was all a dream. The door opened suddenly, and his father and mother were in his bedroom.

'Sleepyhead, let's go to the lake,' his mother said.

Nathan's eyes widened.

'No mama, papa. I will go to school. We can go to the lake on Saturday.'

His mother and father were surprised, but they agreed.

As Nathan's father drove him to school that morning, Nathan promised he would be a good boy, and the water dinosaur would like him.

Brian's Magical Encounter with the Chatty Lizard

Brian was the son of Mr. and Mrs. Scott. Brian had two older sisters and one younger sister. Brian was the only son, so everyone loved him and gave him attention. Brian talked a lot at home, but when he went outside, he kept quiet. He was very shy even though he was five years old.

Saturday was Brian's birthday, and they were going to celebrate it. Brian would be six years old that day. He looked forward to the day, and whenever he was free in school, he would count his hand to know how many days were left.

Miss Samantha was his art teacher, and she left the class when the bell rang for the lunch break. Brian was happy. He spread his hands on the table and counted how many days were left before Saturday. It was just two days. Brian wanted to dance, but he couldn't. He danced a lot at home, but he never danced in class. He had some invitation cards in his bag. His mother told him to give it to his classmates who wanted to come to his birthday party.

Brian loved the invitation card. His mother had allowed him to scribble his name on it, and he had done it neatly too, all by himself. It made Brian proud of himself.

Brian breathed loudly. He usually did that when he was scared. He never talked in class unless the teachers wanted him to. Brian's heartbeat loudly, but he had promised his mother he would give out the invitation card that day.

Brian collected the card four days before that day, and he still hasn't shared it.

'Okay, let's do this,' he told himself. Brian talked to himself whenever he was anxious.

When Brian stood up, his bag fell, and the invitation cards spilled onto the floor. Brian's face felt hot, and he wanted to sit and cry. Brian quickly forgot things. When Miss Samantha was in the class, he had taken his art note out and placed his bag on his lap without closing it.

The class laughed at the cards on the floor. Brian felt sad, and tears came to his eyes. He dashed out of the class. It was his worst day ever.

Outside the class, Brian saw a lizard climbing the wall.

'I wish I were like you,' he told the lizard. 'I would not worry about being laughed at.'

'You will,' the lizard said. Brian's eyes became round. They were as big as huge watermelons. He was surprised to see a talking lizard.

'You talk?' He asked the lizard.

'Of course, I do.' The lizard sighed at Brian. Brian knew that the lizard thought the question was silly, so he asked another one.

'Why would I worry if I was a lizard?' Brian asked.

'Everyone laughs at lizards. They think we're stupid, and little boys throw stones at us.'

Brian suddenly felt pity for the lizard. He didn't know lizards lived such difficult lives.

'But I don't let it bother me,' the lizard said.

'Why?' Brian asked. He talked gently so that the other students that passed wouldn't see him talking to a lizard. They would surely laugh at him.

'Because no matter what you are, people will always laugh anyway,' the lizard said.

Brian's eyes widened, and he thought about it. He watched the lizard crawl away. He imagined that the lizard was the smartest animal in the world.

Brian marched into his classroom. He walked the way he had seen soldiers do on TV. He felt like a big man. As he got into the class, the students began laughing again. Brian didn't mind them. He picked his invitation cards from the floor and shared them out.

Come to my party,

Brian.

Some people read it out, and the class was suddenly quiet. The students looked ashamed. They had made fun of Brian, but he had invited them to his party. They apologized to Brian, and he smiled at them.

On Saturday, Brian had a huge party, and all his classmates were there. They brought him gifts, and he danced with them. Brian was so happy. Brian had taken the advice of the talking lizard, and now he didn't have to pretend to be shy anymore.

Buzzy Bee without a Sting

Once upon a time, in the jungle, there was a family of bees. Mother and father bee had three children. Kampa, Dumei and Somei. They were all girls, and Somei was the second child. Somei was different from other bees in the forest. She had no sting. The sting was the power that bees had against anyone that wanted to hurt them. When other bees were disturbed, they would use their sting against their attackers, but Somei had no sting. Somei couldn't defend herself.

Mother and father bee told Somei not to worry. They defended her whenever they could.

'It would be fine,' they told her.

Somei wanted to believe them, but she couldn't. Somei's sisters would mock her and call her weak, and Somei would cry. She was not allowed to go out alone because she couldn't fight for herself. Somei was very sad. She cried a lot, and she hoped that one day she would have her sting too.

'Weak bee,' Somei's sisters would taunt whenever mother and father Bee were not at home.

'Stop,' Somei would scream.

'Why?' they would taunt.

'I'll tell mother and father,' Somei would say.

'Then we will sting you,' Kampa and Dumei would say. Somei would be scared, and she would cry, but she would not report her sisters.

One day, the sisters had grown up, and their parents were old. Mother and father bee died, and the sisters were sad. Somei was the saddest of all. Her protectors were dead. Her sisters mocked her, and Somei felt very bad.

That week, some humans came to the bush, and they caught three bees. It was Kampa, Somei and Dumei. Kampa and Dumei stung them as they were caught, and the angry men kept them in a box. Somei couldn't sting, and this surprised the bee hunters. They held Somei gently all the way home.

One of the men gave Somei to his daughter as a pet. Kara treated Somei well and loved Somei. She would give Somei a lot to eat and drink and would tell Somei stories about her day.

Somei lived in the house with Kara, and she was now happy.

Kampa and Dumei were made to produce honey all day long. They got tired, but they had no choice.

They would see Somei through Kara's window, and they would feel bad about how they had treated Somei. It was too late, and they couldn't do anything.

Kara and Somei were happy together. Somei forgot about her past and unhappiness.

The Magical Adventures of Daisy, Kelly, and the Enchanting Fairies

Daisy and Kelly are two best friends. They did things together and walked to school together. They loved one another and visited each other's houses.

Daisy and Kelly had something else in common. They both loved singing. They would sing whenever they met, and they both listened to identical records. The two friends would skip on their way home from school, singing loudly in their melodious voices.

When they clocked seven years, they called themselves the best singers in the world. Everyone agreed that they had lovely voices.

'You are not the only ones that can sing,' Brenda said. She was a girl in their class. Brenda had always stared at Daisy and Kelly. Brenda would stare long and hard at them, disliking their voice.

'Yes, we know, Brenda,' Kelly said. Kelly had seen Brenda staring at them before. She knew that Brenda didn't like them.

'But we have the best voices,' Daisy said. She put her hands in her jean pockets and rolled her head from side to side. Daisy had brown hair, and it moved sideways as she swung it. Brenda felt unhappy and insulted. She wished that she had a good voice like Daisy and Kelly's, but she knew she didn't.

'Not as good as fairies!' Brenda shouted. Her voice was loud, and it made everyone in the class go quiet. Brenda felt embarrassed, and she stomped to her seat. Brenda's angry steps were as loud as a moving train.

'Is that true?' Daisy asked.

'What?' Kelly asked back.

'Is it true that we don't have good voices like fairies?'

'Don't mind, Brenda. She is jealous,' Kelly said. Kelly read a lot, and she liked situations where she could try new words. Kelly had learned the word jealous that morning. She was glad to have fit it in the sentence. It felt right.

'But if fairies have better voices, that means we are not the best singers in the world,' Daisy said. It was a thought that could make Daisy cry. They should be the best singers in the world. Everyone liked their voices.

Kelly didn't like it either.

'That's sad,' Kelly said.

'We have to find fairies and see if it's true,' Daisy said.

Kelly agreed. 'We'll have a duet or something. Like in movies.'

They talked about their plans and clapped at their brilliant ideas. It was great, and they were good to go. At the last minute, Kelly remembered something.

'We don't know where fairies are,' Kelly said.

'Oh no!' Daisy groaned. Daisy's face twisted, and she pulled her long brown hair in anger.

'Wait,' Kelly said. She told Daisy about her idea. They would ask their parents when they got home. Then Kelly would go to Daisy's house, and they would go to find the fairies.

The idea was brilliant, and they both loved it.

When they closed from school that day, they didn't sing, and they didn't skip. They went home quietly. They were scared that they might not have the best voices after all.

Daisy asked her mother about where fairies lived when she got home. Her mother's reply was dreamy and happy.

'They live in the woods, of course.'

Daisy was happy. She knew the answer. She waited for Kelly to come.

Kelly asked her mother while eating her lunch of coco pops.

'Fairies?' Kelly's mother asked in surprise. Kelly's mother was a practical woman, and she raised her daughter the same way. 'There are no such things as fairies,' she told her daughter.

Kelly was about to put a spoon of pops into her mouth, but she stopped. She dropped the spoon into the bowl.

'There are fairies, mother,' Kelly said. She pushed out her jaw. Kelly didn't like that her mother was countering her belief.

'There aren't,' Kelly's mother said.

Kelly's lips shook, and she stood from the table. Kelly told her mother that she and Daisy would prove fairies and stumped out of the house.

When Kelly moved closer to Daisy's house, she cleared the tears on her face and smiled. Kelly didn't want Daisy to know what had happened at home.

Daisy jumped at Kelly when she opened the door to let Kelly in.

'There are fairies. Mother said they live in the woods!'

Kelly was glad. She knew she had been right about there been fairies. Her mother just didn't like having fun.

They went up to Daisy's room and planned all they needed for their adventure. They took a torchlight in case it was dusk before they left the woods. They each took a cap to cover their hair, and they headed out of the house.

'Where are you going?' Daisy's mother asked them as she came out of the kitchen, cleaning, and dusting.

Kelly quickly thought of something to say, and she lied that they were only going to the backyard.

'Okay, don't stay there once dusk is setting,' Daisy's mother told them.

The two girls nodded, and Kelly hid the torch beneath her blouse. They walked out of the house quickly. When they were a long way away from the house, they slowed their steps.

'What if we see a snake?' Daisy asked.

Kelly stopped.

'We won't,' she said. It was scary to think they would. Kelly shrugged it off, and they walked on. The sun was bright, and the afternoon breeze blew on the trees gently as they walked into the woods.

They were both excited as they walked on, looking into branches and roots.

'What if we don't find them?' Daisy asked again. She was suddenly full of doubts.

'We will,' Kelly said. After walking for a while, they became tired.

'We should have brought some food along,' Daisy said.

Kelly nodded. She felt hungry also and as tired as if they had been walking for years.

Daisy bent her body and sat on a tree stump.

'Don't sit on my head!' a voice shouted. Daisy jumped up in fright. In her fear, Daisy peed her pants as she gave a loud shout.

Kelly was also scared. They held onto one another in fright and searched for who had spoken.

'What are you tinies doing here anyway?' the voice asked again. There was a little fluttering, and a fairy flew from the tree stump.

'A fairy,' Daisy asked.

'Oh my God, it's a fairy!' they both exclaimed. Kelly felt like she was in a dream. She wished she could take a picture or something to show her mother when she got home. Kelly knew that fairies were real. She had just known.

'Yes, I'm a fairy. My name is actually Rose – like the flower. What are you two doing here?'

'Rose like the flower,' Kelly said. She didn't know there was another rose. Kelly wanted to ask, but the fairy asked them what they were doing again.

'We came to find fairies. We want to know if we have a better voice than fairies,' the girls explained.

Rose crashed to the floor, and there was a small crackling sound.

The girls felt scared until the fairy rose again, and the sound was repeated.

'Are you laughing?' Kelly asked.

'Come with me,' the fairy said and flew ahead of them. The girls walked after her, their thoughts on getting an answer to their question.

They walked for a while before they got to another part of the forest. It was denser and darker. The girls shivered as they followed the fairy. They were scared, but they imagined that the fairy was a good person and they followed.

Rose took them to the other fairies, and the girls watched them with surprise and joy. There were many of them, and when Rose told them why the girls had come, they all began laughing.

Daisy and Kelly felt silly as they stood and waited.

Finally, a fairy who seemed like their queen came out. The fairy was wearing a tiara, and she looked prettier than the other fairies. Her wings were the color of a rainbow. Kelly and Daisy gave their attention to her.

'You got all this wrong,' the queen fairy said. 'Everyone has a unique voice with which they sing. Truly, fairies sing wonderfully, but that doesn't make your voice less wonderful. No one is above anyone, and it's silly that you should think otherwise.' The queen fairy laughed again, and the girls felt stupid for their quest. The queen fairy also warned them not to visit the woods alone anymore.

The queen fairy ordered Rose to take them back home, and when the girls got home, it was dark. Daisy's mother had been searching for them. She was glad to see them.

The girls had learned something from their encounter with the fairy. Everyone was unique. Their voices were beautiful, but it didn't make them better than the next person.

They began to call themselves girls with unique voices but never the best singers in the world. They were happy and contented, and Brenda became happy also.

Welcome to the World, Baby

Mr. and Mrs. Wadley had just given birth to a new child. They named him Jimmy. He had a sister and a brother, Sally and Dante, twelve and seven years old. Sally was the first child, so she was allowed to carry Jimmy more. Their parents often feared that Dante would drop Jimmy because he was younger and a boy. They didn't allow Dante to carry Jimmy as often as he would like. Dante only carried Jimmy when the others were at home.

Dante loved his brother, and many times when Sally carried Jimmy, Dante would play with the baby and make faces at him. Jimmy would laugh. Dante loved how Jimmy laughed. Whenever Jimmy laughed, he would close his eyes, and tears would fall from them. Dante loved everything about Jimmy, and he wanted to be allowed to carry Jimmy often also.

One day, Mrs. Wadley went on a sudden errand to the market. Sally and Dante were at home with Jimmy. They were both doing their homework when Sally remembered something.

'I have to go to Dorothy next door, Dante. I left my note with her. Keep your eyes on Jimmy. Don't let him cry.'

Dante nodded and kept his eyes on his homework. When Sally left, Dante stood from his assignment. He was so happy that his stomach laughed. Dante's stomach would make noise when he was happy, so he called it a laugh. It was his chance to carry Jimmy when no one was around. Dante knew he could do it.

Dante went to the baby who was sleeping in the cot. He looked at Jimmy and smiled. Jimmy was a beautiful baby, and Dante knew that if he could carry Jimmy without dropping him, he would prove the love he had for Jimmy.

Dante's mother didn't allow him to carry Jimmy because she said Jimmy was fat and would weigh him down. Dante didn't mind, though. Jimmy was his baby.

Dante stretched his hand into the cot and pulled Jimmy into his hands. Jimmy shouted, and Dante felt scared. He didn't give up, though. Dante moved Jimmy into his hands and carried him out of the cot. By the time he did that, Dante was sweating. He felt tired. Jimmy was still wailing.

Dante didn't know what to do. An idea came to him, and he went to get Jimmy's feeding bottle. He tried to balance Jimmy in his hands as he took the feeder. Jimmy almost fell, but Dante held on tight. He didn't want his parents and sister to be right about what they thought of him. He would prove to them and Jimmy that he was strong and that he could carry his younger brother.

Dante took the feeder and carried Jimmy over to the couch. He held the crying Jimmy in one hand and put the feeder in his mouth. Jimmy stopped crying and sucked on the empty bottle.

Dante laughed at Jimmy and cleared the tears from his eyes. As Jimmy sucked and nothing came out, he soon gave up and began crying again. Dante wished that Sally would come back. He didn't know what to do anymore.

Dante stood and danced with Jimmy in his hands.

Jimmy, I love you.
I'm trying to prove myself cause I love you.
You are my brother, and I love you.
Watch and laugh as I prove it.

Dante sang, danced, and made funny faces. Jimmy stopped crying and started laughing uncontrollably. Dante didn't worry that Jimmy might think he was stupid. He was happy to make his brother laugh.

Dante turned and was about to sit when he saw his mother. She was standing at the entrance looking at him. Dante was sorry he had broken the rules. He felt sorry.

'Mother, I didn't mean to break the rules,' Dante said. Mrs. Wadley wasn't angry, though. She was happy to see that Dante had not made Jimmy fall. She made cookies for Dante to celebrate with him.

When Sally came back, she was surprised to see Dante carrying Jimmy and eating cookies. Dante was excited as he related the story to her with Jimmy's drool all over his shirt.

The Unruly Mermaid: Ruby's Oceanic Journey

A long time ago, there was a country in the ocean, and in this country, there were many cities. Mermaids lived in the sea, and they were beautiful human fishes with tails. The mermaids have a Queen named Myra and a King named Dystria. The King and Queen had a beautiful princess that they called Pearl. Pearl was a gorgeous baby, and the mermaids in the country loved her.

In another part of the city, there was a little mermaid with a red tail. Her name was Ruby. Ruby was a beautiful mermaid because of her shining red tail. As Ruby grew up, she saw that everyone loved her red tail, and a lot of girls envied the color of her tail. Ruby was the only girl in the ocean who had a red tail. Mermaids had blue tails, yellow tails, pink tails, green tails, and even black tails, but only Ruby had a red tail. Ruby was happy to be unique, and sometimes, people visited Ruby and her mother's house to give them gifts. This made Ruby proud of herself, and she began to act anyhow she wanted.

One night, Ruby's mother, Blue, was lying in bed. She was sick and needed her medications. She was very weak and couldn't get them by herself, so she called Ruby.

'Ruby, I need you to get my medications for me,' Ruby's mother called.

'I'm busy, mommy,' Ruby shouted back. Ruby was in her room also lying down, but Ruby was not doing anything important.

'Ruby, leave whatever you are doing and get my medication, please,' Blue pleaded again.

'Mother, don't be so cruel,' Ruby said. 'I'm polishing my tail; I can't leave it.'

Blue's room was beside Ruby's room. Blue shouted again from her room. 'It won't take a minute, Ruby,' Blue said.

'But the polish will be ruined, and my tail will no longer be good,' Ruby said. Ruby didn't care that her mother was sick, and she kept polishing her tail.

Blue realized that Ruby wasn't going to budge, so she tried to get out of bed to get her medication by herself. Blue fell off the bed and cried out in pain, but Ruby didn't leave her room.

'Are you okay, mother?' Ruby asked from her room.

'I fell,' Blue said. Blue was still lying on the floor, groaning.

'Oh, sorry, ma,' Ruby said from her room.

Blue stood with an aching body and swam over to the living room. She found her medication on the table and took it. Blue used her drugs, and when she went back to bed, she cried for what Ruby had become. Blue cried because Ruby used to be a good and caring girl, but Ruby no longer was. It painted Blue, and she wondered if she had failed in how she brought up Ruby.

The next day, Blue called Ruby and told her she had to change from her evil ways.

'Mother!' Ruby screamed in anger. 'I'm a good person. See, everyone loves me.'

'They love your tail,' Blue told her. 'What if your tail was another color?' Blue asked her.

'You're just mean!' Ruby snarled and went out of the house. She walked around the street. People who saw Ruby waved at her and called her. Ruby soon got to her best friend's house. Her best friend was Amber. When Amber saw Ruby, she hugged her. Amber liked Ruby's tail and would often polish it for Ruby. Ruby cried when Amber hugged her, and she told Amber about what her mother had said. Amber comforted Ruby and told Ruby not to mind her mother.

'She's just old,' Amber told Ruby.

'I know,' Ruby said. Amber and Ruby talked for a while before Ruby went back home. When Ruby got home, her mother told her again that she had to change and flee from bad friends. Ruby was angry and told her mother to leave her alone. Ruby kept on with her disobedience no matter what her mother told her. Until the day she met Princess Pearl.

Princess Pearl decided to take a walk into the city. She was swimming when she saw Ruby. Princess Pearl was amazed to see such a bright red tail.

'Hey, I love your tail. You look so beautiful. I've never seen such a red tail," the princess told Ruby. Ruby had never seen the princess before, but her mother had always told her to respect anyone she saw. Ruby eyed the princess in disgust. 'I know,' Ruby said.

'Can I touch it?' Pearl asked.

'What? Of course not!' Pearl tried to touch Ruby's tail, and Ruby slapped her. Ruby pushed her away, and the princess fell. The soldiers who had been hiding came out, and they carried Ruby. They took Ruby to the palace. The princess was furious about how Ruby had treated her. She commanded the soldiers to place Ruby in the dungeon, and Ruby was beaten. They gave her stale food once a day for three days and beat her every time. Ruby lost weight, and her red tail was no longer shining. After three days, the princess ordered that she should be released. Ruby went home after she was released. People were shocked to see Ruby looking ugly, and they didn't want to move close to her. Many of them mocked Ruby, but Blue pulled her daughter close and hugged her. Ruby regretted disobeying her mother, and she told her mother so. They both cried and rejoiced to see one another again.

From that day, Ruby turned over a new leaf, and when her red tail regained its sparkle, she never boasted about it. She respected everyone, and she was peaceful with everyone around her. Life in the ocean went on as usual, and everyone loved Ruby for who she was.

Taylor's Joyful Comeback

Taylor had just had a rough time in his life. Taylor's mother died and left him with his dad. Taylor's dad is a good man, but Taylor was only five years old, and he needed a mother. Taylor used to be a good and obedient boy before his mother's death, but afterward, Taylor became a shell of himself. He became difficult and rebelled against the rules of the house. Taylor's father would go to work while Taylor went to school, and he would pick Taylor up from school whenever he left work.

Taylor would refuse to eat whatever his father prepared, and he would insist on eating something else, but Taylor's father would not mind, and he would cook whatever meal Taylor preferred. Sometimes, Taylor would be adamant that he wasn't going to school, and his father would get him a babysitter to stay at home with him. Taylor's father was very worried about his son, but he knew it was difficult for Taylor to adapt to his mother's death, so Taylor's father continued being patient and friendly.

Taylor's father would read him bedtime stories at night. Taylor would say that he didn't want to hear it, but his father would continue anyway. Taylor's mother used to read the stories to Taylor while she was alive. Taylor would move to the edge of the bed and cover his ear while his father read him bedtime stories, but Taylor's father was determined.

Taylor was grieving and missing his mother, but he also loved his dad. Taylor was pretending like he didn't care, but he cared a lot.

One night, Taylor's dad began to read a bedtime story to him. Taylor covered his ears like he always did, but he was listening to the story. Every night, Taylor would pretend like he wasn't listening, but he listened because he loved stories. Taylor's father read a story of the tortoise.

In the story, the baby tortoise lost his mother, and he had only his father. Then, the father tortoise told the baby tortoise that he should not worry, that his mother was up in the sky looking at him. Father tortoise told baby tortoise that if he looked up and saw a bright shining star, it was mother tortoise, and she was smiling at baby tortoise. Baby tortoise was happy, and he would look at the sky whenever he missed his mother.

Taylor's father finished reading the story, and Taylor turned to him. Taylor's father was surprised, but he didn't talk.

'Is mother in the sky too?' Taylor asked.

'Of course,' Taylor's father said. Then he said the same thing father tortoise had said. 'When you look up at the sky at night, the brightest star is mother, and she is smiling at you.'

Taylor smiled, and tears fell from his eyes. Taylor's father held him close, and they cried together.

'I love you, dad,' Taylor said.

'I love you too, son,' Taylor's father said. Taylor asked his father to sleep in bed with him that night, and from then, Taylor became a good boy, and he was happy again. Whenever he missed his mother, he would look at the sky, and he would see the brightest star. Taylor's mother kept smiling at him, and he was happy.

Dive into Samuel's Love for Blue

Samuel Jenkins is a six-year-old boy who has liked the color blue ever since he was born. Samuel's parents noticed that Samuel would reject any color that was not blue, and even though Samuel was already six, he still liked the color blue. All the clothes that Samuel had were blue, and he would not wear any other color. Samuel's toys were blue, and his room was also blue.

Sometimes, Samuel would mix blue with white. He ate from blue plates and with blue spoons. Whenever anyone gave Samuel a toy or a gift that wasn't blue, he would scream and throw a fit. He would not accept it. So, Samuel's parents and sister, Sarah, called him the blue boy.

Samuel was going to clock seven on Saturday, which was two days away, and they were all happy. Sarah, his sister, was ten years old, but she had opened her piggy box to get him a gift for his birthday.

On Friday morning, when they woke up, Sarah pretended to be sick, and only Samuel went to school. After dropping Samuel in school, the family went to the mall to get presents for Samuel.

Samuel's mother bought a new pair of shoes, a storybook, and a toy turtle for Samuel, while Samuel's father purchased a scarf and a video game. Everything they both were in the color blue. They also bought wrappings of the same color. When it was Sarah's turn to choose a present for her brother, she saw a toy she liked. It was a flying crystal ball with Mickey Mouse in it. Mickey Mouse was sitting on a chair in the ball and rolling around. It was a beautiful toy, and Sarah wanted to get it for Samuel, but there was a problem. The toy was red.

'Can we get a color blue?' Sarah asked the attendant.

The female attendant laughed and shook her head. 'No. If it's blue, then it's not Mickey Mouse,' she said.

'What will I do then?' Sarah asked her parents, but they didn't know either. Sarah searched for another crystal ball that was blue that she could buy for Samuel, but there was none.

'Sweetie,' Sarah's father said, 'I think you should choose something else for him. Maybe another toy?'

'No!' Sarah shouted. Sarah was close to tears. She had planned to get a perfect gift for Samuel, a gift that he would love, and she knew he only loved blue. 'I'll buy this like that,' she finally said with tears in her eyes.

Sarah's parents looked at her nervously. They were scared that Samuel would reject the gift and hurt Sarah, but they knew there was nothing they could do. They left the mall after paying for what they bought.

Sarah was fidgety as Friday ended, and immediately Saturday came, she quickly got dressed. They all prepared for the birthday. When they were all dressed, Samuel's mother brought the cake she had made. It was a beautiful blue cake, and it made Samuel smile. After cutting the cake, they gave the presents to Samuel. Samuel was excited, and he unwrapped each gift with relish. When it was time to open the gift that Sarah had given him, everyone paused. Samuel, who was unaware, opened the gift. As he saw the crystal ball, his mouth felt open, and his hands shook. Sarah quickly rushed over to him.

'Don't worry,' Sarah said. 'We can paint it blue if you want or something. I can even return it if you don't like it,' she continued.

'Silly,' Samuel said. 'It's beautiful.'

Sarah looked at her parents in surprise before looking back at Samuel. 'Pardon?'

'It's beautiful,' Samuel said again. 'I love it,' he said with tears in his eyes. Sarah was delighted, and she hugged Samuel.

From that day, Samuel would take the crystal ball to school and everywhere he went. Everyone saw that he loved it, and then Sarah and her parents started buying Samuel beautiful things that were not blue, and he loved them.

Samuel began to like objects that were not color blue, and he no longer fussed when people gave him gifts that were not blue. He wore yellow, pink, and red clothes, ate from colorful plates and he liked them. They still called him blue boy, though, because blue remained his favorite color.

Jay and Jack

Jack lives on a sleepy street in a small house with his grandmother. Jack is seven years old, and he has a dog that he named Jack. Jack's dog would also answer whenever Jack's grandmother called him, so Jack shortened his dog's name to Jay.

Jack loved Jay a lot, and they would walk everywhere together. Whenever Jack's grandmother sent him to the store that was down their street, Jay would follow him. Jack loved Jay very much, and Jay loved Jack too. Jay also slept in Jack's bed at night. They were best friends.

Suddenly, when Jack woke up one Thursday, Jay didn't wake up with him as he usually did. Jack thought it was a joke, and he shook Jay's body, but Jay didn't stand up. Jack moved closer to him, and he noticed that Jay's eyes were closed. Jack panicked, and he rushed to his grandmother's room. Jack didn't knock on the door before he ran in, but his grandmother was already awake.

'Jack! What is wrong?' Jack's grandma asked. She was sitting at her desk with glasses on and writing on paper.

'Grandma! Jay is not waking up,' Jack wailed.

'What?' Jack's grandmother followed Jack as he ran out of her room. When they got to Jack's room, Jay was still lying on the bed.

Jack's grandma went to the dog, and she touched his body. She noticed that Jay was breathing, and he was shivering.

'He's alive, Jack,' Jack's grandma said. 'He's just sick.'

'Really? Will he be fine?' jack asked.

'Yes. We will get the doctor to come and see him, okay?'

'Yes, ma,' Jack said.

'Now, go and get ready for school,' Jack's grandma told him.

'Can I stay with Jack, please? Please, grandma.' Jack's lips trembled, and he was about to cry. Jack's grandma looked at him with pity.

Jack was scared his grandma would say no, but he wanted to stay with Jay. Jack had lost his parents just the year before, and that was why he was living with his grandma. He was scared that Jay would die too, and he would have no best friend.

'Please, grandma,' Jack said again. Tears were falling from Jack's eyes.

'Okay, you can stay with him,' Jack's grandmother told him. Jack was thrilled. Jack cleared the tears from his eyes.

'Thank you, grandma,' Jack said quickly. Jack hugged his grandma's legs, and he ran to his room.

Jack stayed with Jay all day. The doctor came to see Jay, and he treated Jay. Jack stood with Jay all through. He only left Jay when he wanted to eat, and that was because Jack's grandmother didn't want him to eat in his room. Jack laid next to Jay on the bed and held him close. Jack told Jay not to worry, that Jay would be fine.

The next day also, Jack didn't go to school. Jack cared so much for Jay the same way the doctor did. At noon, Jack's grandmother wanted him to go to the store to get her some jam. Jack refused because he wanted to stay with Jay.

'If you don't give him breathing space, he won't get well,' Jack's grandma told Jack.

'The drugs won't work?' jack asked.

'Yes, it won't,' Jack's grandma said. Jack was afraid. He quickly went to get what his grandma wanted. From that moment, Jack limited his presence to Jay. He wanted Jay to get well, and he was willing to do anything. He checked up on Jay often, but he didn't linger there with him.

On Sunday morning, when Jack woke up, Jay woke up at the same time too. Jay barked joyfully at Jack. Jack was happy to see that Jay was well again. Jack hugged Jay. He ran with Jay to his grandma's room. Jack's grandma was also glad to see that Jay was doing well. They continued giving Jay his medications until Jay became very well again. Then Jack and Jay began to walk around together again, and they were both happy.

Lola's Furry Friend Fun

Lola had always wanted a pet, a dog preferably, but Lola's father didn't buy one for her. Lola would ask her mother too, and her mother would just shrug and tell Lola to leave her alone.

Lola didn't like that her parents were like that. She saw her friends at school, and they all had pets. Lola was the only one who didn't have any pets. Even Cecilia, who was the smallest in Lola's class, had a goldfish as a pet. Cecilia would tell the class how her goldfish had made bubbles in the water and lay still to make them think she was dead. Another classmate of Lola's, Franca, had a greyhound dog that was cool and gentle, and she talked about him all the time. It made Lola feel jealous. Lola had nothing to talk about, except school, her home, and her parents, which was not even special.

'Mother! I have to get a pet! Maybe a goldfish like Cecilia, or maybe a greyhound like Franca, or maybe even a housefly. Just buy me one pet,' Lola pleaded with her mother. Lola had just come back from school, and Lola's bag was still on her back. Franca had told them in school that day that her dog was very good at playing catch. This had made Lola decide that she would beg her mother very well that day. Lola told herself that she needed a pet like her mates. Any kind was acceptable.

'I can't get you a pet now. Tell your father,' Lola's mother said.

'But mother! Father won't answer me,' Lola said.

'Why do you want a pet?' Lola's mother asked. They were in the kitchen. Lola's mother was preparing lunch for the family.

'Cause all my friends at school have pets,' Lola exclaimed.

'That's not enough reason,' Lola's mother said. 'You don't want something because other people have it too. You should have a reason,' Lola's mother said.

'You and father are just mean,' Lola said. Lola marched out of the kitchen. When Lola got to her room, she threw her bag on her bed and laid down on the bed. Lola knew there was no way she would convince her parents to get her a pet if she didn't have a good reason. Lola wondered what she would do. Then, an idea occurred to Lola. Lola decided that she would construct a good reason that would make her parents buy her a pet.

Lola was happy with her idea. Lola took out her jotter from her bag. Lola wrote out in her clear writing. Reasons I want a pet, and she underlined it. She decided that she would begin compiling reasons for her parents. Lola decided that she would list at least five reasons for her parents by asking her friends why they had their pets.

At lunch break in school the next day, Lola went to search for Franca. She found Franca playing on the swing on the playground.

'Franca, why do you have a pet?' Lola asked Franca. Franca stopped playing and got down from the swing.

'Well, Grey is not just any pet,' Franca said. Franca held her head up and continued. 'Grey is my favorite dog, and I have him because I love him,' Franca said.

'Thank you,' Lola said. Lola went to a shade in the playground. She took out her jotter and wrote in it.

Reason one: I want a pet because I love pets.

The next person Lola went to look for was Cecilia.

'Cecilia, why do you have a pet?' Lola asked when she would find Cecilia.

'I have a pet because they are fun to be with,' Cecilia said.

'Thank you,' Lola said. Lola went to a quiet spot and wrote in her jotter.

Reason two: I want a pet because pets are fun.

Next, Lola went to meet John. John was also Lola's classmate, and John had a cat for a pet.

'John, why do you have a pet?' Lola asked.

John was making a sandcastle. He looked up from the unfinished castle and answered Lola.

'I have a pet because I can talk to her when I'm sad. Even though Kitty doesn't talk back, I know she understands me,' John said.

Lola thought it was a very brilliant answer, and it would make a good reason for her list.

She thanked John and left.

Reason three: I want a pet because pets are understanding, and I can talk to my pet when I'm sad.

Lola read her list and smiled. She was progressing, and she hoped that she would be able to finish before the break ended.

The next person Lola went to meet was Lizzy. Lizzy had a frog that she often bragged about. Lola thought it was weird to have a frog for a pet, but Lizzy never seemed to mind, and Lizzy liked talking about her frog.

'Lizzy, why do you have a pet?' Lola asked.

'A pet? Oh, you mean Fred? Well, Fred makes me happy,' Lizzy said.

'Thank you,' Lola told Lizzy. Lola felt like a grown-up as she wrote the next reason in her jotter.

Reason four: I want a pet because it would make me happy.

Lola reread her list, and she felt like dancing. She had only one reason to make it complete. She thought about who she should ask. Then she remembered Drake. Drake had a nightingale. Drake would always tell them how beautiful it was and how it sings and makes him happy.

Lola started looking around for Drake, but she didn't find him.

'Franca, have you seen Drake?' Lola asked.

'No, I haven't,' Franca said. Lola asked all around, but no one had seen Drake. Lola was getting sad. She wanted to complete the list that day so that she could show her parents. When she didn't find Drake, she decided to go back to class. When Lola stepped into her classroom, she found Drake sitting at his desk. He was writing.

'Drake!' Lola screamed, unable to hide her excitement. 'I have been looking for you since!'

'Why have you been searching for me?' Drake asked as he raised his head.

'I want to ask you a question,' Lola said. 'Why do you have a pet?'

'Oh, I've never thought about that before,' Drake said. Drake's response made Lola pause. No one had said that to her. All the classmates she had questioned had answered immediately. Lola sat down beside Drake as he thought about it.

'Well, people have pets for different reasons. I have my pet because I wanted her. When I saw Gina, she looked sad, and I just liked her and wanted her. I didn't plan to have a pet, but I wanted Gina and told mother to buy her for me,' Drake said.

Lola stared at Drake. She couldn't talk. Drake's answer was thoughtful, and Lola liked it.

'Thank you very much,' she told Drake and stood up from his desk. Lola went to her seat and looked at the jotter. She stared at it and wondered how she would write what Drake had said.

Reason five: I don't need a reason to have a pet. Pets need someone to love them, and that is all the reason I need.

Lola read her list, and she smiled. She loved the last reason best, and Lola thought if her parents do not understand that, then there was nothing else she could do.

After closing that day, Lola went home jogging. She was excited for her parents to see the list and buy her a pet. Lola thought about which animal she would choose. She thought about it as she skipped home. Lola thought she would prefer a dog or a cat.

Lola wasn't watching the road. She suddenly tripped over a tree branch and fell. Lola yelped, and as she screamed in pain, another voice yelped in pain too. Lola looked around but saw no one. She stood up from the ground and dusted her body. Lola was glad to realize she wasn't hurt. The voice yelped again, and Lola looked around the tree branch that had caused her to fall. Lola saw a little dog. The dog had its left leg under the huge branch. Lola felt pity for the creature, and she used her might to roll the tree away. The dog removed its leg and fell to the floor.

'Sorry,' Lola told the dog. 'I hope you're not too hurt. Where did you come from?'

The dog stared at Lola with sad eyes. Lola looked around, but there was no one on the road.

'Your dog is here!' Lola screamed. She placed her hands beside her mouth to make her voice louder. A woman poked her head from the window of a house close to where Lola was standing.

'Shut up and go home,' the woman said and went back inside.

Lola dropped her hands and looked at the dog.

'Go home,' she told the dog and began walking away. The dog followed Lola, and Lola pursued it, but the dog didn't go back.

The dog followed Lola home, but Lola didn't let it in.

'Mother, I'm home,' Lola called out.

'Welcome Lola, how was school?' Lola's mother greeted her. Lola's mother was in the living room watching TV.

'It was fine. Mother, can I get a pet now?' Lola asked.

'Hmm, do you have a good reason now?' Lola's mother asked back.

'I have five good reasons,' Lola said. Lola's mother was surprised.

'Tell me then,' Lola's mother said.

Lola brought out her jotter from her bag and opened to her page of reasons. Lola gave the book to her mother.

'Wow,' Lola's mother said. 'I love the last reason best.'

'I love the last reason best too,' Lola said.

Lola's mother looked at Lola and smiled. 'We can get a pet for you now,' Lola's mother said. Lola jumped up in excitement. She hugged her mother and screamed.

'Thank you, ma,' she said. 'Hooray! I can have a pet now, too,' Lola said happily.

'We still have to talk to your father,' Lola's mother said. Lola didn't answer. Lola knew that whenever her mother agreed about something, her father would agree about it too.

A loud tap suddenly sounded at the door, and Lola and her mother went to check it. They found the dog Lola had rescued. Lola told her mother how she had helped the dog, and Lola's mother was proud of Lola.

'Can I keep her then?' Lola asked her mother.

'If we don't find the owner, yes.'

Lola danced excitedly.

When Lola's father returned from work, Lola showed him her list of reasons and the dog she had found. He was proud of Lola, and he told Lola so. Lola's father agreed that Lola could have the dog if they don't find the owner.

Lola's parents searched for the person that owned the dog, but they didn't find anyone. Lola's parents posted fliers about the dog also, and no one came to claim it. After a week, Lola's parents told her she could have the dog. Lola was glad. Lola named the dog Love, and she was happy to have a pet at last. She loved Love and would always want to be with her dog.

Beauty's Fairy Friends

Beauty loves fairies, and her mother reads her stories about them. Beauty is five years old, but most of the bedtime stories she listened to had to do with fairies. Sometimes, Beauty would imagine that she was a fairy, and sometimes, Beauty would imagine that she met a fairy.

Beauty's parents were Mr. and Mrs. Smith, and they loved Beauty very much. Beauty loved her parents too, and she was a good girl at home. Mr. and Mrs. Smith liked to go fishing every weekend, and they would take Beauty with them.

On one such outing, Mr. and Mrs. Smith took Beauty as usual. When they got to the lake, it was hot in the afternoon, and Beauty was already dozing. Mr. and Mrs. Smith spread a blanket for her to sleep on. Beauty laid down on the blanket and slept off.

When Beauty woke up, her parents were beside the lake talking and fishing. Beauty sat up on the blanket, but Mr. and Mrs. Smith didn't notice that Beauty was awake. Beauty looked around and saw a butterfly on the blanket. It was a beautiful butterfly. Beauty wanted to touch it. As Beauty reached her hand to touch the butterfly, it flew into the air. The butterfly didn't fly far away from Beauty, so Beauty reached for it again, but the butterfly moved out of reach. Beauty stood up and followed the butterfly as she tried to catch it, and it moved away from her.

Beauty kept following the butterfly, and she didn't realize it when she walked into the woods. The butterfly got tired of playing with Beauty and flew away. It was then that Beauty decided to go back. As Beauty walked around the woods trying to get back to her parents, she got lost more. Beauty wandered around the woods in fear, but she didn't find her parents or the spot they had been at.

Beauty became scared, and she hoped her parents would find her.

'Mama?' Beauty called. She began to cry. Beauty was scared because she was alone in the woods, and no one was with her. 'Papa?' she screamed again, but nobody heard.

Beauty was walking, shouting, and screaming around the forest, but there was no response. Beauty began to feel tired, and she sat on a tree stump. The forest was cool, but it was also full of insects, and they bit Beauty. Beauty felt miserable, and she wished she could go home.

Voices approached Beauty's side of the forest, and Beauty stood up from the tree with fear. Her lips were shaking, and she was beginning to feel the cold of the woods affect her.

'Who is there?' Beauty asked as the voices got louder. Beauty was scared, and she didn't know if she should run. She also didn't know where to run to, so she stood where she was, hoping that it was not an animal and that it was someone who could take her to her parents.

A group of flying creatures suddenly appeared, and Beauty's eyes widened.

'Fairies?' Beauty asked herself in surprise.

'Isn't that a girl?' One of the fairies asked the other. Beauty counted four fairies in all.

'It is,' another fairy replied. The fairies moved closer to Beauty. The fairies all had different colors. There was a blue, yellow, green, and red fairy.

'What are you doing here?' The green fairy asked.

'I was following a butterfly, and I got lost,' Beauty told the fairies. Although Beauty was sad that she was lost, she was happy that she had met fairies. Beauty was relieved that it was not an animal, and she was glad to see colorful fairies such as the ones her mother always read to her in her stories.

'These children!' The blue fairy said. The blue fairy sounded tired as she said it. It seemed that many children usually got lost from following butterflies, and the fairies usually had to help.

'It's always the butterflies,' the yellow fairy said.

'Where were you before you got lost?' The green fairy asked.

'With mama and papa at the lake,' Beauty said.

'Okay, let's get you back to them,' the green fairy said. Beauty watched the fairies as they flew in the air. The four fairies flew ahead of Beauty, and she followed them.

The fairies took her to the exit of the woods, and after telling Beauty not to follow butterflies, they told her to go. When Beauty walked out of the forest, she found her parents walking from the other side.

'Beauty!' Mr. and Mrs. Smith screamed when they saw Beauty. The three of them hugged. Beauty burst into tears while her mother carried her and consoled her.

Mr. and Mrs. Smith were glad to see Beauty safe and sound. They packed their equipment and left for home.

As they drove home, Beauty thought about her encounter with the fairies and smiled. She had not liked getting lost, but she had enjoyed meeting the fairies. She decided she would tell her mother about the fairies when they got home.

Larry's Awesome School Adventure

There were a lot of things that four years old Larry liked. He liked chocolates, strawberries, candies, and biscuits. Larry loved eating, playing, listening to music, and dancing. Larry was happy to be at home most of the time with his mother, playing with her.

After Larry clocked four years, Larry's parents told him he would start school. Larry cried and told his parents he didn't want to go, but Larry's parents said he had to go to school.

The day that Larry was supposed to go to school, he became sick. Larry's temperature was very high, and this made Larry's parents worried. Larry's parents took Larry to the hospital, and the doctor gave Larry treatment and medication. The doctor told Larry's parents that Larry had to stay in the hospital for a while because Larry's fever was very high, and it would not be safe for Larry to go home yet. Larry's parents were worried about Larry. They took turns staying with Larry at the hospital.

After the first night at the hospital, Larry's parents made sure that Larry was attended to by many doctors. Larry's parents were wealthy, and they wanted to make sure Larry got well at all costs.

By the third day when Larry was discharged, Larry had lost weight, and he was exhausted. Larry did not like the hospital experience. Larry was not allowed to eat chocolates, and they didn't let him play, and music had hurt his head. When they got home, Larry's parents did not disturb him. They allowed Larry to rest.

After a month, Larry had almost forgotten about school. He was once again his old self, happy and playful. Larry's parents did not forget about school, and they decided to remind Larry that he had to go to school. Larry's parents had bought all the items that Larry would need in school.

'Larry, you have to go to school tomorrow,' Larry's mother said that night.

Larry's face became sad. 'But I don't want to go,' Larry said.

'But you have to go,' Larry's father said. 'School is important.'

Larry's lips shook. 'Then, I'll fall sick again,' Larry said.

'Then you'll have to go to the hospital again,' Larry's mother said.

Larry squeezed his face. He did not like the hospital. Larry knew there was nothing else he could do. He could not fall sick because he didn't want to go to the hospital.

The next day, Larry went to school with tears in his eyes. Larry's mother dropped him in the school. Larry met boys and girls of his age, and he made friends with them. When school ended, Larry was happy, and he loved school.

The Tale of the Wealthy Tortoise

A long time ago, animals used to walk like humans. In the jungle, animals loved one another and helped one another too. Elephant was the King of the animals, and the animals loved him because he treated them well. The richest animal in the forest was not the elephant. It was the Tortoise.

Tortoise was very rich, and he was more prosperous than King Elephant. Tortoise had many clothes; he had a lot of servants in his house. Tortoise lived in a huge house that was even bigger than the King's. Tortoise was so rich that people would go to him for help and assistance. In the beginning, Tortoise was generous, and he gave to people willingly. Then a time came when Tortoise became proud.

Tortoise would refuse to help people who came to him for help, and sometimes, Tortoise would mock them before he helped them.

One day, Rabbit went to Tortoise to ask for monetary help. Rabbit explained that his family was hungry, and he needed money to feed them. Tortoise laughed in Rabbit's face.

'I don't have money to give you,' Tortoise said. 'Go and work for your money too,' Tortoise said. Rabbit pleaded with the Tortoise, but Tortoise told his guards to send Rabbit out of his house. Rabbit went to King Elephant, and Elephant helped Rabbit.

Tortoise was very sure of his wealth, and it made him happy. One day, Tortoise went on a journey. Tortoise was gone for four days, and when Tortoise returned, all he met was the burnt remains of his house. Tortoise servants had left, and there was no one to ask. When Tortoise asked the other animals how his house had been burnt, they shrugged and walked away. Rabbit passed, and Tortoise asked him.

'Maybe your servants became tired of your pride and burnt it,' Rabbit said and walked away.

Tortoise sat on the floor and cried. He wished he had not been proud. All the money he had was burnt with the house. No one wanted to help Tortoise, and there was nothing for him to do. Tortoise remembered that he could sell the produce on his farm. When Tortoise got to his farm, the farm had also been burnt. All of Tortoise farm produce was gone. Tortoise felt horrible. Tortoise went to King Elephant and narrated the ordeal to him. King Elephant ordered that they should search for Tortoise's servants because they had to be the culprits. They searched all around, but they didn't find any of Tortoise's servants.

Tortoise was regretful of his actions. He wished he could turn back time and be a better person, but he couldn't. Tortoise became the poorest person in the jungle. Tortoise was mocked and jeered at, and he could not do anything. Tortoise became humble because all his money disappeared. Tortoise had no choice but to act as a servant for other animals so that he could eat. This was how Tortoise learned the most bitter lesson of his life.

The Brave Dragon's Unexpected Journey

There was a time before humans; dragons lived on Earth. The Earth was just a large forest at that time. There were no houses, no streets, no vehicles. There were only dragons and trees. There were different kinds of dragons; some had different colors while some could fly. Some could only walk. All these dragons could do one thing, though. They all spit on fire. Whenever the dragons got angry, they would open their mouth, and fire would come out of it. The dragons also used the fire to burn trees that would make them warm during the winter. The dragons cared for one another, and they lived happily.

The second Mother Dragon became pregnant, and she gave birth to a little dragon. She named him Red because he was very red. When the other dragons saw Red, they loved him because he was beautiful.

Then the time came for Red to walk, but he didn't. Everyone knew that Red should be walking already, and they told Red, but whenever Red tried to walk, he would fall.

'Walk Red,' the dragons would say. Red would stand and try to walk, only to fall again. It was a huge shame for Red. The dragons realized that Red was crippled. Red couldn't walk. They saw that it was not that Red didn't want to walk. Red wanted to walk, but Red couldn't.

'A crippled dragon!' Some of the dragons said. 'That is such a shame. He is an embarrassment to us,' the dragons said.

'I feel pity for him,' some other dragons said. Those dragons were good, and they wished they could help Red to walk.

Red was sad. He was the only dragon who could not walk. Red would sit by himself while everybody moved around, and he would stare with envy. Red wished that he could walk too, but he couldn't walk no matter how Red wished for it.

'Don't worry, Red. It doesn't matter to me that you can't walk. I love you all the same,' Red's mother would tell him.

When the dragons were asleep, Red would crawl into a deep part of the forest and cry.

For a while, Red mourned his inability to walk. Then, one day, Red became tired. He had been crying for so long, but it was not helping. Red decided to make the best of his disability.

Red went into the bush again while the dragons were sleeping. Red did not go to cry this time. Red went to uproot a tree. Red used fire from his mouth to make the tree fall. Then he used the fire to divide the tree into different sizes. After this, Red used his sharp claws to carve the wood. Red carved and carved until he formed a dragon. Red carved the First Mother Dragon. The First Mother Dragon is the first dragon to give birth.

Red crawled back to the part of the forest where the other dragons were. When the dragons woke up in the morning, they saw the image that Red carved.

'Who made this?' They asked one another. Nobody could answer because they didn't know. Red was still sleeping then, and nobody imagined that it could be him. They thought Red was useless because he couldn't walk.

When Red woke up, he looked around and saw that the dragons had made a platform for his sculpture. Red looked at it and smiled.

'Don't you think it's beautiful?' Red asked a dragon beside him.

'It is wonderful,' the dragon said. 'First Mother loved it, and she was the one that ordered that we should place it where we could all see it,' the dragon told Red.

Red smiled in excitement. He was thrilled that the dragons loved his work.

'We just don't know how it got here or who made it,' the other dragon said sadly.

Red felt terrified. He assumed the people would have known that it was him.

'Why? It's me!' Red exclaimed loudly.

The dragon looked at Red in surprise. 'Are you serious?' the dragon asked Red.

'Of course,' Red said again.

'Wow!' the dragon said. The dragon was amazed that Red had made the sculpture. 'Red made the image!' the dragon hooted for the other dragons to hear.

All the dragons immediately gathered around Red, and he explained how he had gone out at night to make the sculpture.

The dragons were amazed, but some of them didn't believe Red. So, Red told them to get him wood, and they did. Red started carving, and the dragons watched him. Red carved and carved, and before he was done, the dragons were amazed because they knew what Red was carving. Red was carving himself! When Red finished, the dragons believed him, and they were surprised that a crippled dragon had such talent.

Red became very sought after, and many dragons would ask him to carve them. All Red would ask for would be wood, and he would carve their image perfectly well that it would please and surprise the dragons.

Some dragons became jealous of Red and the attention he got. Those dragons no longer thought of Red as an ordinary cripple. They wanted to be like him. They went to the bush and cut trees and tried carving as Red did, but no matter how they worked and tried, they never got it right. Those dragons were forced to respect Red, and they went to him to teach them how to sculpt.

Red became popular, and the time when he had cried and thought of himself as an ordinary cripple ended. Red became happy.

Thomas and His Singing Journey

Immediately Thomas began talking at a year old; Thomas knew he wanted to sing. When Thomas was four years old, he would go around the house screaming songs that he had listened to. Thomas loved music, and his parents always got him albums to listen to. Thomas had his favorite songs, albums, and artists.

Thomas began school, and he made friends. One day, Thomas and his classmates were asked what they would become in the future. Thomas said he wanted to become a singer. The class laughed at Thomas. The other students said they wanted to be doctors, lawyers, bankers, and so on. When Thomas got home, he felt sad. He did not listen to music like he usually did after school.

'Mum, is it a bad thing to become a singer?' Thomas asked his mother.

'No baby, it is not, and you will make a famous singer someday. You have the best voice in the world,' Thomas's mother told him.

'My friends at school laughed when I said I want to be a singer.'

'Oh no, baby. It's because they don't understand. Sing for them in school.'

'Okay,' Thomas said. Thomas felt happy about it. He could help his mates understand that singing was good. Thomas loved singing, and his mother said he had the best voice. Thomas believed it, and Thomas believed he could be one of the best singers in the world when he grew up.

In school the next day, Thomas tried to sit still in class. He was excited about singing for his classmates. Thomas had never done it before. He has never sung to his classmates before. When the bell rang for a break, and the teacher stopped teaching, Thomas quickly went to the front of the class.

'Hi everyone,' Thomas said. Everyone stopped to look at Thomas. They were curious and wanted to know what Thomas had to say. 'I want to sing for you so that you know that singing is a good job,' Thomas said.

Thomas's classmates looked at one another. They didn't know how to act, but they were attentive to Thomas anyway.

Thomas sang one of his favorite songs. It was a slow song that Thomas's mother also loved. As Thomas sang, some of his classmates that knew it also sang along. It was exciting, and when the song ended, they all loved it. They clapped for Thomas, and they said he would be a good singer when he grew up.

Thomas was happy.

When Thomas got home, he told his mother how his friends had liked to hear him sing. Thomas's mother was happy.

'You can always choose to stand, Thomas, or you can choose to run,' she said.

Thomas was glad that he didn't run and let his classmates misunderstand his dream. He smiled at his mother as he looked forward to when he would be a grown-up singer.

Bill, the Marvelous and Charming

On Hillary Street, there lived a family of five people. There was Mr. White, Mrs. White, Lily, Susan, and Bill. They were a family that loved one another. Lily was the oldest child, and she was ten years old. Susan was eight and Bill was five. When Mr. and Mrs. Smith first gave birth to Bill, they looked at him with love. They loved him immediately. When Susan and Lily saw Bill, they were shocked.

'He is ugly,' they had both said.

'Sweeties, he is not ugly,' Mrs. White had told them.

'He is beautiful like you two,' Mr. White had said.

The girls had nodded and agreed, and from that day, they had called Bill beautiful. Other people around would see Bill and squeeze their faces, though. Whenever they saw Bill, they would say he was ugly. Mr. and Mrs. White, Lily and Susan would both fight on Bill's behalf.

'Bill is beautiful,' they would all argue. Everyone on Hillary Street had to accept, like the Whites, that Bill was beautiful.

When Bill clocked four years, he had to resume school. Mr. and Mrs. White enrolled Bill in the same school that Lily and Susan attended.

On the first day of school, Bill's classmates stared at him. There was a boy in Bill's class who was the oldest. The boy's name was Steve, and he was six years old. Steve would bully Bill because he was older and bigger than Bill.

'Look at you, ugly boy,' Steve would say. It made Bill angry, but Bill couldn't do anything.

'How was school today?' Bill's family members would ask, and Bill would not be able to talk.

Every day at school, the students were mean to Bill.

'Ugly, ugly, ugly,' they called him. Bill would hide his head under his desk and cry.

Whenever Bill got home, his parents and sisters would praise him. 'Beautiful Bill,' they would say. 'So beautiful.'

One day, Bill could not take it anymore. When his classmates started to call him ugly, Bill remembered how his parents and sisters believed he was beautiful, and Bill stood up.

'I am beautiful,' Bill shouted. The class became quiet, and they all watched Bill.

Bill had never defended himself, and this made his classmates surprised.

'I am beautiful,' Bill said again. Bill stood up from his desk and went to the front of the class. He raised his shoulders and walked like a peacock as he displayed himself. 'Every day, I am beautiful,' Bill said. Bill's voice was firm as he talked. He didn't cry this time.

'Who said so?' Steve asked, trying to be mean again.

Bill stared hard at Steve. 'I said so, about myself,' Bill said. Steve could not talk. No one could say anything. Bill had just told them that what he said about himself was what mattered, and they just watched him.

After school, that day, Bill's family asked him how school was.

'It was beautiful,' Bill said, 'like me.'

His parents and sisters hugged him and praised him. When Bill slept that night, he dreamt of the sky and the stars, and they were just as beautiful as Bill.

Brave Richard's Fearless Journey through the Dark

Richard is a boy of six years old who is good and generous. Richard helped at home and in school, and he was nice to everyone. Richard was also brave. His father taught him how to ride a bicycle, and Richard got injured many times, but Richard did not give up until he could ride it.

In school, Richard did not allow anyone to be cheated. Richard was the biggest in the class, so whenever anyone tried to bully the smaller ones, Richard would protect them. Richard had a lot of friends in his neighborhood and school. They all loved him.

Despite the fact that Richard was big and scared of no one, Richard was scared of the dark. Richard would beg his parents to keep the light on whenever he slept at night. He would be unable to sleep whenever it was dark, and he would be afraid that something would come to get him in the dark.

Richard's parents were glad to leave the light on for their wonderful son, but they wanted to help him to get over his fear too. At first, Richard's father did not agree with Richard's mother.

'He will grow out of it when he gets older,' Richard's father said.

'He won't. I was like him when I was small, and I did not grow out of fear. I'm still scared of the dark, Richard's mother said. 'We have to help him.'

'Okay,' Richard's father finally said. He had no choice but to agree.

Richard's father and mother planned, but Richard wasn't aware of it.

One day, when Richard closed at school, the school bus picked Richard and dropped him at home. Richard walked into the house, and he met both of his parents at home. It was unusual, and it surprised Richard.

'Dad, why are you at home?' Richard asked his father.

'You don't want your dad around?' Richard's father asked back. Richard smiled, but he didn't answer. Things felt wrong to him.

'We want to have family time,' Richard's mother said. 'With lots of fun.'

'And games,' Richard's father echoed.

The family ate lunch together, Richard's parents assisted him with his assignment, and they played board games.

When it was night, they ate dinner before Richard's parents announced the actual game they had in mind.

'To the main fun of today,' Richard's father said and brought out three pairs of night-vision goggles from a bag.

Richard stared curiously at his parents. 'What is this?' Richard asked.

'They are called night vision goggles,' Richard's mother said. 'They are used to seeing in the dark,' she told Richard.

Richard laughed at his parents. 'But we have light and our eyes to see at night,' Richard said.

Richard's father shook his head. 'It doesn't work that way, Richard,' he said. 'This is a game. We switch off the lights and wear the googles.'

'Switch off the lights?' Richard asked. 'But we can't switch off the light. I don't like the dark.'

'Sure, baby,' Richard's mother said. 'That's why we have the goggles.'

Richard was scared of the dark, but he was excited about the game. Richard loved games a lot.

'What game will we play?' Richard asked.

'Hide and seek,' Richard's mother said quickly.

Richard loved hide and sought, so he agreed to play the game with his parents. Richard's parents switched off the light and told him not to wear the goggles until they asked him to. They went into hiding and told Richard to look for them. Richard searched around in the dark house using his goggles to see, and he was able to find his dad but not his mum. Then Richard and his dad searched for Richard's mother. They found her after exploring all the house. It took a long time before the game ended for the night. Richard felt terrible that it had to end, but Richard's parents assured him that they could play the game every night. Richard was happy.

After a month, Richard's parents decided to test if Richard was still scared of the dark. When they kissed Richard goodnight, they switched off the light in his room. Richard just smiled at them in the darkness and said nothing. Richard's parents were glad. Their plan had worked.

Richard was no longer afraid of the dark. He had played a lot with his parents in it so that he was comfortable in the dark.

From that day onward, Richard slept with the light off, and he had beautiful dreams.

Carla's Woof-tastic Talking Dog Adventure

Carla was a young girl of five years who loved animals. Carla's mother was a veterinarian, so this was also one reason Carla loved animals. Carla lived on a ranch with her parents, and her father also reared animals on the land. Carla liked to think of herself as a cowgirl, and she would often ride on a horse with her father or her mother, and they would race with the wind.

Carla imagined that she would grow up and become a veterinarian like her mother or a rancher like her father. She loved animals a lot.

Carla would go to her mother's workplace after school and watch whatever patient her mother had for the day.

'What animal is this?' Carla would ask if she had not seen the animal before. Her mother would tell her, and she would memorize the name of the animal in her head.

If Carla's father picked her up from school, he would take her home, and Carla would follow him around the ranch asking questions.

'Has Spirit given birth?' Carla would ask about the pregnant horse that they had, and Carla's father would respond.

Whenever their teacher asked them to narrate stories at school, Carla would always have the most stories to tell. They were always exciting stories, and many times during lunch break, Carla's classmates would crowd around her and beg her to tell them stories about her animals. Carla would tell them the newest story with delight.

One day, Carla was waiting for any of her parents to pick her up from school. Carla's parents didn't always tell her who would pick her. Sometimes, her father showed up, and sometimes, it was her mother.

On this day, Carla was waiting outside the school for any of them when she heard a howl nearby. Carla's eyes widened. She had enough experience with animals to know when an animal was in distress.

Carla went around the school, and she found a dog. It was a Labrador lying down on its side. Carla felt sympathetic and moved to the dog.

'What happened to you? Are you hurt? Where did you come from?' Carla asked.

'I'm Lucy. I live several streets away. My right leg hurts: I think I hurt myself there,' the dog said.

Carla's eyes widened as she heard the dog talk. Carla has met many animals, both from her mother and father, and none of them had ever spoken in the human language.

'You are talking!' Carla said. Carla was surprised.

'Yes. My leg hurts. Will you help me?'

'Sure,' Carla said. Carla was still surprised as she moved to the dog's leg. She saw a thorn stuck into it. It was wedged deep. Carla pulled the thorn out, and Lucy, the dog, shrieked in pain.

'I've removed it,' Carla said.

'Thank you,' Lucy told Carla.

'Do you always talk?' Carla asked Lucy.

'No,' Lucy said. 'I talk only when I want to. Most times, we prefer to use the dog language which humans call bark.'

'Do you mean all dogs talk?' Carla asked. She was shocked indeed. No dog had ever talked to her before.

'Yes,' Lucy said. 'Thank you once again,' Lucy said and ran off.

Carla watched Lucy go. When Carla's mother arrived, Carla was still surprised about the talking dog. Carla decided she would try to get her mother's dog patients to talk to her. Carla bounced in the car from excitement.

When Carla got to her mother's office, though, the dogs merely looked at her when she tried to talk to them. They refused to speak.

Carla decided that she might never meet another talking dog. So, she held the memory of Lucy, the talking dog dear to her. She would never forget her encounter with Lucy.

Dive into Fun with Bob's Swim Lessons

When Bob clocked six years, he could ride a bicycle perfectly well. Bob had other hobbies that he performed well. Bob was also a good dancer. There was something that Bob could not do. Bob could not swim. Bob had a sister and a brother. Bob's brother, Carl, was a terrific swimmer, and his sister Mandy was good at swimming too. Bob wanted to be a good swimmer also, but whenever Bob walked into the water, he would get scared and run out.

One day, Bob's mother hired a swimming instructor for Bob.

'Bob, I just hired someone that will teach you how to swim,' Bob's mother told him.

'Why?' Bob asked.

'So that you can learn to swim,' Bob's mother said.

'I'm scared of the water,' Bob said. Bob was about to give up on swimming because Bob's parents, his sister, and brother tried to teach him several times, but it didn't work.

'I know. Miss Semina is a professional. She will be able to teach you,' Bob's mother said.

Bob felt excited. If Miss Semina could teach him to swim, he would be a very happy boy.

'When will Miss Semina come?' Bob asked.

'On Monday,' Bob's mother said.

Bob danced with joy. His school was vacationing that day which was Friday. That meant Bob could learn to swim in three days.

On Monday morning, Bob woke up elated. Bob ran to his mother's room.

'Mom, Miss Semina is coming today!' Bob shouted.

Bob's mother and father laughed at his excitement.

'She's coming by ten,' Bob's mother said. When they looked at the time, it was still seven o'clock. Bob went to have his bath and tidy his room. When Bob finished, it was still nine o'clock.

'It's taking so long,' Bob told his mother. Carl and Mandy laughed at Bob.

'She'll be here soon,' Bob's mother told them. Bob's father had gone to work. Bob's mother gave them tasks to do. She gave Bob a coloring book to work in, and Bob passed the time with that.

A car drove into their compound at ten o'clock. Bob heard the sound and raised his head from his book.

'Is that her?' Bob asked his mother.

'It should be her,' Bob's mother replied. Bob's mother was reading a book on the sofa. She stood up and placed the book on the chair. Bob's mother, Bob, Carl, and Mandy went to the compound, and they welcomed Miss Semina.

Miss Semina was a beautiful woman with dark hair and a wide smile. Bob liked her immediately. Bob's mother introduced Bob and his siblings to Miss Semina. Miss Semina smiled at them and told them she was pleased to meet them.

Bob's mother took Miss Semina to the pool while the children followed. When they got to the pool, Bob and his siblings changed into their swimming wear. The water of the fool had been drained for the children. Mandy and Carl jumped into the water, but Bob could not. Bob stared at them with envy while he stared at the water with fear. Miss Semina also jumped into the water.

'Come on, Bob. Come into the water,' Miss Semina said. Mandy, Carl, and Bob's mother watched Bob.

'I'm scared,' Bob said.

'Why?' Miss Semina asked.

'I can drown,' Bob said. Bob was standing at the edge of the pool, but he did not step into the water.

'We are in the water, Bob. Are we drowning?' Miss Semina asked.

'No,' Bob replied.

'Good. Come into the water, Bob. Do you trust me?'

Bob looked at Miss Semina. He was scared, but Miss Semina smiled at him. Miss Semina stretched her hand to Bob, and he took it. Then, Miss Semina pulled Bob into the pool. Bob was scared, but Miss Semina just held his hand and stood in the pool with him. When Bob realized, Miss Semina was not going to force him to swim, Bob relaxed.

That day, Miss Semina did not tell Bob to swim. Miss Semina and Bob just walked around in the pool. After that day, Bob was more comfortable with being in the water.

Miss Semina continued helping Bob throughout that week.

By Friday, Bob could wade through the pool by himself without any help. Bob and his siblings were happy. Bob could finally swim.

Join Raya as She Makes a New Friend at School

Raya is a five year old girl who liked being by herself. Raya did everything alone in school. She had no one to talk to and nobody to play with. Raya's mother would tell her to make friends at school, but Raya was very shy. The big boys and the girls in class would bully Raya and make fun of her. Raya would not mind them. Raya would sit by herself and let them say whatever they wanted. After a while, they all left Raya alone. They did not mock her anymore, but Raya felt very lonely.

One day, Raya was in school eating lunch. Raya ate slowly and quietly. Raya did not talk to anyone. Then, a girl walked to Raya.

'I am Sheila,' the girl introduced herself. The girl was new to the school.

Raya looked up at the girl. She had just finished eating her lunch when the girl came to her.

'I am Raya,' Raya told Sheila.

'I want to be friends with you,' Sheila told Raya.

Raya looked at Sheila in surprise. No one had ever told Raya that they wanted to be friends with her. It was a big surprise to Raya, and Raya did not know how to react.

'Okay,' Raya told Sheila.

Sheila laughed. Sheila had noticed that Raya was sitting alone, and Sheila had thought that Raya must be lonely. That was why Sheila had gone to meet Raya and wanted to be friends with Raya.

Sheila playfully drew Raya out of her seat. Raya followed as Sheila took her to the playground. Sheila and Raya took turns playing on the swing. Sheila would push Raya, and when Sheila was tired, Raya would push.

Raya and Sheila had so much fun, and they were so happy together. Raya looked forward to going to school every day and meeting Sheila. Raya was no longer lonely, and she had a friend she could play with and talk to every day.

Soaring with the Bird That Couldn't Fly

A long time ago, the mother bird laid some eggs. Mother bird laid her eggs at the root of a tree. Mother bird laid nine eggs in all that she was pleased with her eggs. Mother bird guarded her eggs against other animals. The mother bird would sit on her eggs daily to give them warmth so that they could hatch and become birds.

Mother bird sat on her eggs every day, and she would only leave the eggs when she was looking for food to eat. One day, while mother bird was sitting on her eggs, a loud sound started coming from the eggs. Mother bird was glad. She stood up from the eggs to watch them. The eggs were beginning to hatch. It thrilled mother bird to see her young birds. The eggs hatched one after the other until there were nine birds. The mother bird was happy, and she welcomed her birds into the world.

Out of the nine young birds, there was a strange bird. The bird looked different from the other birds, but when mother bird saw the bird, she didn't mind. Mother bird thought that the bird would grow up to look like her sister bird too.

Mother bird would cover the nest with grass whenever she was looking for food. Mother bird did this to protect her young ones. Mother bird acted like this every day and would bring food for her children.

The eight birds who looked alike would look at their sister with curiosity.

'Why don't you look like us?' they would ask.

The strange bird who didn't look like them would shrug. She didn't know why she didn't look like her siblings. Mother bird also didn't know. So, they all decided not to worry about it. They lived happily together.

Then it was time for the birds to start flying.

'I will teach you to fly today,' mother bird told her young ones.

They were elated, and they jumped around happily.

The mother bird made the nine birds stand together on a line, and mother bird showed them how to move their wings to fly. Three birds got it right and were able to fly, but they fell when they were in the air.

Mother bird kept teaching them daily, and when it was a week, all the birds could fly a short distance except the strange bird. The ninth bird could not fly, and she was not happy about it. The ninth bird felt bad enough that she did not look like her sisters, but it was worse that she could not fly.

Mother bird tried to teach the ninth bird to fly, but no matter what, the bird could not lift her big body into the air.

One day, while the mother bird was trying to teach the ninth bird to fly, another family of birds passed by. They were walking and moving their bodies left and right.

'Look, mama!' one of the young birds is called mother bird. 'See, those birds are not flying.'

Mother bird looked at the birds, and she was surprised. 'Why are you not flying?' mother bird asked the other family of birds.

'We can't fly,' the other birds said. 'Our wings are for jumping over high borders, not for flying. We are chickens, not real birds.'

Mother bird and her young ones were surprised. They had never heard anything like that before.

'Why does that bird look like us?' the other family asked when they saw the ninth bird that could not fly.

'Can she fly?' the other family asked again.

'I can't fly,' the ninth bird told them and started crying.

'You should not cry,' the other birds said. 'You are not a bird. You are a chicken.'

Mother bird was surprised, but she had to let the ninth bird go and meet her new family because that was where she belonged. They said goodbye to the ninth bird, and the ninth bird left with her new family.

The ninth bird no longer had to pretend to be a bird. She was no longer strange, and she looked like her new siblings.

Whenever the mother bird was flying with her children sometimes, they would see the ninth bird with her new family and wave at her. The ninth bird would wave also. The ninth bird was no longer jealous, and she no longer wished that she would fly because she knew that she was not a bird and she was not born to fly.

Splish, Splash, and Play with Jane!

Jane lived in a cottage in the countryside. Jane lived in the house with her mother and her sister Kary. Jane was four years old while her sister Kary was six years old. They were close, and they played together and went to school together. Their mother always took them to school.

After school, Jane and Kary would do their homework, and then sometimes, they would help their mother plant flowers in the garden. Sometimes, Jane and Kary would just sit in the garden, and they would play and look at the beautiful flowers in the garden. The garden had several flowers with beautiful colors of blue, red, pink, purple. The garden was Jane's favorite place in the house. Often, when Kary was in the house doing her homework, Jane would take her homework into the garden to do.

Spring arrived, and it was the season for rain to fall.

'Do not go to the garden every day,' Jane's mother told Jane and Kary. 'Limit your visits to the garden, and whenever you notice that rain is about to fall, you should leave the garden and come into the house. Do you understand?' Jane's mother asked her daughters.

'Yes,' Jane and Kary replied.

Then one afternoon, after Jane came back from school. Jane's mother and Kary were taking a nap. Jane was supposed to be napping also, but Jane didn't feel sleepy, so she went to the garden. It was cloudy that afternoon, but Jane wanted to see the flowers, so she went to the garden. When Jane got there and was looking at the flower, it began to drizzle. Jane thought she would just look at the rest of the flowers and rush inside, but the rain started to pour heavily.

Jane saw no reason to go inside anymore because she was already wet. Jane danced in the rain and smelled the pleasant honey smell of the flowers. After Jane was satisfied with her play, she walked inside. When Jane walked inside, Jane met her mother sitting in the living room. Jane's mother was surprised to see Jane coming from the rain. Jane's mother had thought that Jane was in her room with Kary and that they were sleeping.

'Did you go to the garden?' Jane's mother asked Jane.

'Yes,' Jane said. Then Jane sneezed, and Jane started trembling.

Jane's mother was very disappointed in Jane. Jane had disobeyed her rules and gone into the rain, and Jane had caught a cold. Jane's mother took Jane to her room and took off the wet clothes. She clothed Jane in dry clothes and gave her some cold syrup. After this, she made Jane lie down in bed.

Throughout that week, Jane was sick. Jane could not go to school, she could not see the garden, and she could not play. Jane would watch Kary do everything that she could not do, and she would feel sad. Jane promised herself that she would never play in the rain again. Disobeying the rules was not good, Jane thought.

Emerald and Loveth's Fantastic Friendship

Emerald and Loveth are close friends who loved one another. They were both in the same class, and they were both six years old. Emerald had dark hair while Loveth had shining red hair, but aside from this, the two were alike and loved the same things. They listened to the same songs and sang the same pitches. Their houses were also beside one another. Emerald and Loveth were like twins, and they sat beside each other in class.

Lydia was also a student in Emerald and Loveth's class. Lydia was a big girl in the class, and she usually bullied the weaker girls. Lydia had tried to bully Emerald and Loveth many times, but she had failed. Emerald and Loveth would stand for each other and would never allow anyone to bully them. Lydia didn't like this, so she looked for how she could separate Emerald and Loveth.

Then one day, Emerald brought her mother's makeup kit to school. Emerald just wanted to show Loveth and her other classmates how it looked like. Emerald could also apply it on her face, and Emerald showed them how to do it. Loveth wanted to try it, and Emerald allowed her, but Emerald did not allow any other person to touch the palette. Lydia was a bad girl. Lydia got angry that Emerald did not allow her to try the powder.

When it was time for lunch break, everybody left the class to play. Lydia also left the class, but Lydia went back to the class when she knew no one there would be. Lydia took the powder palette from Emerald's bag, and she broke it. After breaking it so that it would not be useful again, Lydia put the makeup kit in Loveth's bag. Then Lydia went back to the playground to play.

After the break, the students returned to their class. After the art teacher walked into the class and Emerald was searching her bag for her note, Emerald noticed that her mother's makeup kit was gone. Emerald was scared, and she began to cry. The art teacher saw Emerald crying, and she became worried.

'Why are you crying, Emerald?' The art teacher asked.

'I brought my mother's makeup kit to school. I did not tell my mother, but now it's gone,' Emerald said.

Loveth was sitting beside Emerald. Loveth felt pity for Emerald, and the other students who had also used out of the makeup felt pity for Emerald.

'You should not have taken your mother's belongings without her permission,' the art teacher told Emerald.

'Yes, ma. I won't do it again,' Emerald said. 'But I have to find it. It's gone,' Emerald said as tears fell from her eyes.

The art teacher was a nice woman who did not like seeing her students sad, and she decided to help Emerald find the makeup kit.

'We will search everybody's bag,' the art teacher told Emerald.

Emerald nodded, and they started the search. The art teacher wanted to start with Loveth because Loveth was sitting beside Emerald, but Emerald told the art teacher that Loveth was her best friend and could not steal from her.

The art teacher and Emerald searched all the bags but did not find the palette. Then the art teacher said they had to search Loveth's bag and find the makeup kit there.

Loveth and Emerald were shocked. Emerald looked at Loveth in surprise and hurt.

'I did not expect you to steal from me,' Emerald said, crying. 'And you broke it too!' Emerald said.

'I did not do it,' Loveth said. Loveth was crying too, and she was sad.

The art teacher did not know what to do. The other students were also quiet. They did not want Emerald and Loveth to fight because Emerald and Loveth were best friends.

'It was Lydia who broke it and put it in Loveth's bag,' a small voice said. All the students looked at the person that spoke. It was Ben. Ben was a small boy who did not talk much in class.

Ben stood up. 'I saw Lydia when she came back to the class during break. Lydia took Emerald's makeup kit and broke it,' Ben told the class.

Everybody was shocked that Lydia would do such a bad thing.

'You are a bad person,' Emerald told Lydia.

'I'm so sorry,' Emerald said to Loveth. Emerald and Loveth had tears in their eyes, and they hugged each other. Loveth had been scared that she would no longer be friends with Emerald.

Lydia apologized for what she did, and the art teacher took Lydia to the Proprietor. They called Lydia's parents, and Lydia's parents had to buy another makeup kit for Emerald.

Emerald and Loveth forgave Lydia for the wrong thing she did, and they thanked Ben for helping them. Loveth and Emerald continued to be friends, and they trusted one another more than before.

The Magical Bond of Bella and Her Adorable Cow

Bella lived on a farm with her parents, Mr. and Mrs. Henry, and her siblings Tom and Jenny. Bella is five years old, and she was a good girl. Everybody on the farm loved Bella because she was such a sweet girl. Bella liked living on the farm. Bella enjoyed playing with the horses they reared on the farm, and she also loved the dogs that her father had.

Jenny showed Bella how to milk the cows and comfort the horses whenever they were in pain. Bella liked the chore of milking the cow, and she would follow Jenny to milk them every morning. Bella's parents did not allow her to milk the cows herself, though. They said that Bella would not handle it because the cows were impatient, and Bella would be slow.

Then one day, Mr. Henry bought a new cow. When Mr. Henry showed the cow to his family, they were pleased to see it. Bella was the most excited. Bella loved the cow immediately, and she named her Mimi. Mimi was different from the other cow that they had. Mimi was gentle and patient. Bella would go to see Mimi every day, and she would talk to Mimi.

Mimi became Bella's favorite animal, and Bella felt that Mimi listened whenever she talked. Then, it was time to get milk from Mimi. Mr. and Mrs. Henry told Jenny to milk Mimi. Bella argued and said she could try it, but her parents refused.

'You are too young to milk a cow,' they told Bella.

'But Mimi is different,' Bella said. Bella's parents refused. So, Bella followed Jenny to Mimi's shed.

'I wish they would let me try,' Bella said when Jenny started milking Mimi.

'I think she's more patient than the other cows,' Jenny said.

'Why don't they want me to try then?' Bella asked her sister.

'Because they are worried about you. They don't want you to get hurt,' Jenny told Bella.

'I won't get hurt,' Bella said. Bella felt that she should be allowed to try it before they decided.

'Okay, come and try it,' Jenny told Bella. Jenny stood from the stool and told Bella to sit. Jenny showed Bella how to place her hands and pull the milk. At the first trial, Bella did not get it right, and she used more force. Bella finally did it, and she milked Mimi. Bella was proud of herself, and Jenny was also proud of her.

Jenny and Bella went back to the house, and they ate breakfast and went to school. After this day, Jenny allowed Bella to milk the cows, but their parents were not aware of it.

One day, while Bella was milking, Mr. Henry walked into the shed and found Bella sitting at the stool talking with Jenny. Mr. Henry was surprised.

'What?' Mr. Henry shouted.

Bella stood from the stool immediately, and Jenny was also ashamed of what they had done. Mimi was the only one unmoved by the noise.

'But I said Bella was not to milk the cows,' Mr. Henry said to Jenny.

Jenny stared at her father and confessed what she and Bella had been hiding. 'Bella has been milking the cows for a month now, father, without any disaster,' Jenny told her father.

'Wow. Are you certain?' Jenny's father asked.

'Yes,' Bella and Jenny replied. Jenny's father smiled, and he told them to continue. Jenny's father walked out of the shed. Jenny and Bella were thrilled. They hugged one another, and Bella could now milk her favorite cow without fear.

The Daring Rescue of the Dying Dinosaur by Jerry and Pals!

Jerry, Kyle, Bob, and Carmen were four friends who lived on the same street. Jerry was the oldest among them, so he often acted like the leader.

The four friends loved the same stories, and their favorite fantasy animal was the dinosaur.

'But are dinosaurs real?' Carmen asked her friends one day.

'Yes, they are,' Jerry said. Jerry's friends trusted him and accepted his answer as final.

The four friends loved going to the forest to play, and they would often go there after school. They usually go to the woods with a few weapons like knives, bows, and arrows to protect themselves in case something terrible happened.

One day, while the four of them were playing in the woods, they heard a loud shrill sound coming from within the woods. They were scared because it had never happened before.

'We should leave,' Bob said immediately. Carmen and Kyle nodded. They agreed with Bob that they should leave the forest.

'No! We should check,' Jerry said.

'But it could be a lion looking for food to eat,' Bob said again. Bob was scared already, and he wanted to leave the forest.

'It's not possible. That sound is like the sound of pain,' Jerry said.

'The sound of the pain of hunger,' Kyle said.

'Okay,' Jerry told them. 'You can all leave. I will find out the cause of the noise alone.' Jerry took out his knife and looked at his mates.

Carmen sighed. She could not leave Jerry alone in the forest. She joined him and took her knife in her hand also. Bob and Kyle joined, and Jerry nodded at them, and they moved further into the forest holding their weapons. As they moved into the deep woods, different sounds were heard. Crickets, birds, and rodents were making different sounds. The four friends were scared, but they marched on. They used their knives to cut the branches that got in their path.

'Where is it?' Bob asked.

'We don't know where the animal could be,' Carmen said.

'Wait,' Jerry said. Suddenly the shrill came again and they paused. The sound was coming to their right, and they moved in the direction. When they got there, they met a wounded animal.

'Oh no! It's a dinosaur,' Carmen exclaimed. The others saw it also, and they were all surprised and excited. It was their first time seeing a dinosaur, and they were thrilled to see it. The dinosaur gave a shrill again.

'I think it hurts,' Jerry said. The dinosaur was lying by its side on the ground, and it had its eyes closed. It was brown in color and huge. The four friends turned the dinosaur around with their strength as they looked for where the dinosaur was hurt. They saw a gaping wound on the other side of the dinosaur.

'It must have been shot,' Jerry said. 'How do we help it?'

'Perhaps, we should get some first aid items and help it until it gets well?' Carmen advised.

'Is that wise?' Bob asked.

'I think it is,' Jerry said. 'We can't take it to the hospital, can we?'

They all agreed that Carmen's decision was wise. They marked the spot where the dinosaur was and covered the dinosaur with some leaves. They went to Carmen's house and got some first aid equipment before going back to the forest.

The four friends administered first aid on the dinosaur and bandaged the wound. They covered the dinosaur with leaves when they are later left it in the forest. The four of them would visit the dinosaur daily and treat the animal. It took six days before the dinosaur got well.

On the seventh day, when Jerry, Kyle, Bob, and Carmen got to the spot where the dinosaur was, they did not find it there. They were confused, and they wondered if they were in the wrong location, but the mark they had placed on the spot was still there. They looked around but did not see the dinosaur.

'Maybe it left?' Bob asked.

'Or maybe it was a dream,' Carmen teased and smiled.

Suddenly, there was a swooping sound, and the dinosaur was on the floor beside them. The four of them had not expected it, and they all jumped back in fear brandishing their weapons. When they saw it was the dinosaur, they hid back their weapons. The four friends were hesitant, and they did not know how to act with the dinosaur since it was now healed.

The dinosaur moved to them, and they caressed the dinosaur.

'Thank you,' the dinosaur told them.

The friends were surprised. They had not known that the dinosaur could talk. They played with the dinosaur, and they were happy that they had saved its life.

The dinosaur left the forest, but sometimes, the four friends and the dinosaur would meet in the woods and play together.

Remarkable Village of Brave Girls

Once upon a time, there was a village. In the town, only male children were allowed to rule the kingdom. In this village, though, the King and the Queen were giving birth to female children alone. They had no male child at all. This made the King and the Queen sad because they had no child to rule them when they were gone.

The four princesses were sad too. The first princess was Sara, the second princess was Kara, the third princess was Lara, and the fourth was Mara. The princesses had a meeting where they discussed the situation of the kingdom.

'Females should be allowed to rule too,' Sara said. 'I should be able to rule my people,' Sara said.

'Certainly,' Kara said.

'I don't see why females can't rule,' Lara said. 'Wisdom is not limited to any gender.'

'We have to do something. We have to prove that we can do this,' Mara said. The princesses wanted a chance to prove that they could rule. If Sara were a male child, there would be no discussion before she would be chosen as the next crown prince, but she had to prove her worthiness because she was a female.

Sara, Lara, Kara, and Mara trained themselves to be strong. They prepared themselves to fight and also equipped themselves with knowledge about the kingdom.

One day, the chance to prove themselves came.

The neighboring village came to fight with Sara's town. Sara and her sisters changed into attire of war when they heard the sound of the fighting outside their palace. When the King saw them, he panicked, and he told them to go back to their rooms because females were not allowed to fight. Sara and her sisters ignored their father, and they joined their father in fighting.

Sara immediately went to the leader of the other village, and she fought with him. She dodged his sword and hit him with her sword until she conquered. Sara and her sisters fought vigorously at the battle, and they won. The warriors of the other village ran away, and Sara's village won.

The villagers were surprised, and all decided that Sara was fit to be King after her father. They all agreed that Sara had proven that she could defend her kingdom.

Sara and her sisters were happy. The rule of having a male child to rule the kingdom has been conquered. They could now rule their kingdom.

The Exciting Trip to Grandma and Grandpa's House

Dylan has always lived in the city with his parents. They lived in a huge house that has several modern facilities. Dylan is the only child, so he usually had no one to play with at home except his parents. Dylan's parents got a babysitter for him whenever they were not around, and Dylan would play with her sometimes. Usually, Dylan played with his toys. Dylan had a lot of toys. He had dolls, trains, and car toys. Dylan also had airplane toys, and he loved each of his toys.

When Dylan clocked five years old, Dylan's mother gave him a speaking doll. Dylan loved it very much, and Dylan named it Bill. Dylan let Bill sleep with him at night, and Dylan would wake up in the morning with Bill beside him.

At five years old, Dylan had seen a lot of the city, but Dylan had never been to the countryside. Dylan looked forward to going to the countryside someday because Dylan's father often read Dylan stories of how the country was quiet and peaceful.

One day, Dylan's parents told him they would visit Dylan's grandparents. Since Dylan was born, Dylan had never seen his paternal grandparents physically. Dylan's maternal grandparents lived in the same city with them, and they often visited them, but Dylan had never seen his father's parents. Dylan often saw them when Dylan's parents made video calls with his grandparents. Dylan knew that his grandparents lived in the countryside, so Dylan was excited about the visitation. Dylan would finally get to see the countryside, and he would also see his paternal grandparents.

Dylan's parents told him that they would leave for the countryside in one week and they would be there for three weeks. They could stay that long because it was summer vacation, and Dylan's parents were also taking a break from their work.

Dylan was thrilled by the idea and every other thing his parents told him. To Dylan, it would be a great adventure and a way to see another view of the world.

Dylan waited impatiently for the day they would travel. It was to be a Saturday, and they would go in Dylan's father's car. Dylan was anxious to see his Pa and Ma Jackson.

'Dad, when are we going?' Dylan asked his father one night at dinner.

Dylan's father chuckled as he took a gulp of water.

'It's tomorrow,' Dylan's father told him.

Dylan's eyes popped out. Dylan had been counting the date, but Dylan had lost count the day before. 'Tomorrow!' Dylan screamed. Dylan stood up from his seat and did a quick dance.

'Dylan! Sit down and eat your meal,' Dylan's mother said. Dylan's mother was laughing too.

Dylan sat down and continued eating his meal. Dylan rushed his meal so that he could finish quickly and prepare for their travel the next day.

'Calm down, Dylan,' Dylan's father said. Dylan's parents could see that Dylan was excited, and Dylan was rushing his meal. Dylan was forcing himself to calm down and sit still.

When Dylan finished his meal, he helped his mother to clear the table. Dylan followed his parents to their room.

'Why are we not packing yet then?' Dylan asked his parents.

'We'll pack tonight,' Dylan's mother said. Dylan's mother followed Dylan to his room, and she began taking the clothes and other materials that Dylan would need. Dylan followed her in excitement, making sure not to get in her way.

'Do you want to pack anything else?' Dylan's mother asked him.

'Yes!' Dylan said, remembering his toys. Dylan took several toys into the bag that his mother had given him, but Dylan did not put Bill in the bag because he would sleep in bed with Bill. Dylan's mother packed all that Dylan would need, and Dylan's father also came to Dylan's room. Dylan's parents read him a bedtime story and kissed him goodnight.

Dylan hugged Bill close to him and waited for morning to come.

Dylan's mother woke him up the following day, and immediately Dylan woke up; he was excited. It was the day they would travel to see his paternal grandparents. They got ready and started on the journey.

Dylan sat in the back seat with Bill in his hands while Dylan's parents sat in the front. Dylan watched the scenery that flashed past them as they drove. Dylan was looking forward to seeing his grandparents.

When they moved close to the countryside, Dylan gazed at nature with an open mouth.

'So many trees, mom, dad,' Dylan said. 'It's so beautiful.'

'Yes,' Dylan's mother and father agreed. They got to a small house that was overlooked by a garden.

'Is this it?' Dylan asked as they got down. Dylan's parents told him it was, and Dylan was impatient as his parents got their luggage from the car. Dylan helped his mother to carry his bag of toys, and they marched to the door.

Immediately they got to the door, the door swung open, and Pa and Ma Jackson were at the door. Dylan's grandparents hugged his parents before they both stared at him. Dylan suddenly felt shy, but Ma Jackson pulled Dylan close, and Dylan hugged her legs. Pa Jackson carried Dylan in his arms and hugged him. Dylan felt happy to see his grandparents.

Pa Jackson took Dylan fishing every morning, and he taught Dylan how to fish. Ma Jackson also made unique dishes for Dylan to try, and Dylan loved them.

Dylan enjoyed his three-week holiday with his grandparents, and when the three weeks ended, he was reluctant to leave. When it was time to go, Dylan was looking forward to his next visit to Pa and Ma Jackson.

The Sun and Moon's Mysterious Secret

Once upon a time, the sun and the moon were inseparable friends. They were both in the sky at the same time. The sun and the moon would both be in the sky during the day and at night. The sun and the moon talked a lot, and they liked to be together. People would enjoy the sunshine and the moonlight at the same time. It was beautiful, and the people in the world at that time loved it.

Then one day, people started arguing.

'I think the sun is better than the moon,' one man said.

'The moon is better,' another man said.

'It would be better if the moon appeared alone,' one woman said.

'The sun is terrible and harsh,' another woman said.

The sun and moon watched as people said all these things. The sun got angry that the women were mean to him, and the moon got angry that the men were cruel to her.

'I know I'm better than you,' the sun said.

The moon was hurt, and she spoke angrily at the sun.

'I am better than you,' the moon said. 'You are harsh, and I am cool. The reason people are able to enjoy every time is because of me. They like you because of me. If they had only you, they would die,' the moon said meanly.

The sun was furious. The sun felt betrayed, and he wanted to hit the moon. The man of the sky who ruled the sky decided to interfere. He had been watching the sun and the moon accuse each other before, but he stopped them when he saw that they were about to fight.

'Stop!' the man of the sky said.

'He started it,' the moon said.

'It's your fault,' the sun said. The sun and the moon started to insult each other again.

'Stop!' the man of the sky shouted. The sky was getting dark and cloudy because of the fight between the sun and the moon.

'The two of you should not fight,' the man of the sky said. 'Learn to be at peace,' he told the moon and the sun. The moon and the sun nodded, and the man of the sky left them alone.

Immediately the man of the sky left, the moon hisses at the sun.

'You are useless in the sky,' the sun retorted.

'Your usefulness is not seen,' the moon said. They began to trade insults again, and the man of the sky came back. The man of the sky saw that the moon and the sun could not work together anymore, so he decided.

'You will have to work separately,' the man of the sky said.

'Better!' the moon retorted.

'I can't even work with her anyway. She gives me a headache,' the sun said.

The man of the sky sighed. The sun and the moon were causing him so much trouble. 'Okay then,' the man of the sky said. The man of the sky waved his big golden wand, and he commanded that the sun and the moon would never see each other again.

'You sun will rule by day,' the man of the sky told the sun. 'Moon, you will rule by night,' he told the moon and waved his wand.

From that day onward, the sun was only seen during the day, and the moon came out at night. The moon and the sun never became friends again, and they never saw each other again.

Jake's Fun Toy Adventure

Jake is a little boy who lived in a small house with his mother and his grandmother. Jake loved the little house, and Jake loved his grandma and his mother. Jake's mother and grandmother loved him also.

Jake attended a small school in the neighborhood, and he was a good boy who helped others; and Jake was also attentive in class. The people in the area loved Jake, and whenever Jake's mother was taking him to school, the people in the neighborhood would call out to Jake and wave at him. Jake's mother was a poor woman, but she worked hard and took care of Jake and her mother.

All the children in the neighborhood had at least one toy each, but Jake had none. Jake wanted a toy, but Jake did not tell his mother because Jake did not want his mother to worry.

One day, Jake was reading a storybook in school when a bigger boy than he came to collect the book. The boy, whose name was Henry, was six years old, and Jake was just five years old. The storybook belonged to a girl in Jake's class. The girl's name was Angelina. Angelina saw as henry snatched the book from Jake's hand and ran outside. Angelina was worried, and she wanted to cry. She knew that Henry was a bully, and Jake could not collect the storybook back from Henry.

'Don't worry, I will get it back,' Jake said. Jake went to their class teacher, and he reported Henry to her. The class teacher made Henry return the book, and she punished Henry for causing trouble for Jake and Angelina.

Another day, while Jake was waiting for his mother to come and pick him from school, a classmate of Jake, Robert, who used a wheelchair, wanted to go out of the class. Robert was tired, and he found it difficult to wheel himself out because the class teacher was not around. Jake helped Robert push his wheelchair, and Jake waited with Robert until Robert's mother came to pick Robert.

There was another day while Jake was playing around in the neighborhood with his friends. One of his friends Carl, who also lived on Jake's street, fell and got injured. Jake was the only one that did not laugh at Carl. Jake helped Carl stand, and Jake took Carl to his mother, and Jake's mother helped Carl treat the wound. It was after that that Jake took Carl to Carl's house.

Jake was good to all his classmates, and he helped them whenever he could. Jake never worried about what his mother could not get him.

Then, Jake's birthday was approaching. Jake was excited because this meant his mother would get him something new. Jake wondered what his mother would get for him.

On the day of h birthday, Jake's mother and grandma woke him up, and they wished him a happy birthday. Jake's mother had baked him a beautiful cake, and Jake loved it. The three of them ate some of the cake before Jake left for school, and Jake's mother kept the remaining cake in the fridge.

When Jake got to school, everyone in his class and his class teacher sang a birthday song for Jake. Jake felt happy, and he danced.

Then, they all gave Jake a present. Some gave Jake pencils, erasers, handkerchiefs, and Jake was happy as he collected the gifts. After everyone had given Jake the gifts, the class teacher told Jake that they wanted to give him something else.

'What is that?' Jake asked the class teacher. The class teacher smiled, and Jake's classmates smiled also. Jake looked at them and wondered what it was they wanted to give him.

'Your mates have been saving some money to get you a gift together for your birthday. They want to use it to thank you for all that you do for them,' the class teacher said. 'They all saved together and got you this gift.' The class teacher brought out a wrapped gift, and when Jake unwrapped it, he found a big toy car that could move on its own.

Jake was pleased and excited. 'Thank you,' Jake told them.

'We love you,' they told Jake. Even Henry said it too.

When Jake got home, he showed his mother the toys he had gotten, especially the toy car that thrilled him most. Jake's mother was also happy for him.

'It's a reward for being good,' Jake's mother said. Jake was glad that he was always acting good because now Jake also had a toy.

The Daring Adventure of Juliet's Hard Choice!

Juliet lives with her parents in a busy neighborhood. Juliet attended a school that she loved, and Juliet had a lot of friends in school too, but school was vacationing soon. Juliet loved singing and drawing. Juliet's parents bought her a sketch board and a karaoke machine. Juliet was also learning to play the piano. After school, Juliet would either sing or draw; usually, Juliet did both. She loved doing the two, and they were Juliet's hobbies.

As the time for school vacation drew near, Juliet's parents asked her to choose where she would like to spend the holiday. They gave Juliet two options. Juliet could spend it with her father's parents or her mother's parents. Juliet was excited about the possibilities. Juliet's maternal grandmother was an artist. She could draw and paint, and she made terrific paintings. Juliet loved visiting her. Juliet's paternal grandfather was also a musician. He could sing, play the piano, he was good at playing the guitar, and he had produced a lot of albums. Juliet loved visiting him also.

Juliet was confused. Juliet did not know who to choose for the visit.

When Juliet's best friend Sandy came to visit Juliet, Juliet told Sandy about the options her parents had given her.

'I think you should go to your grandfather,' Sandy told Juliet. 'You like singing more than you like drawing, so you would enjoy it more if you went there,' Sandy said.

'But I like doing the two equally,' Juliet argued.

Sandy shrugged and told Juliet to think about it and make the decision she liked.

Juliet asked her favorite doll, Jasmine, about the options, but Jasmine did not say anything. Jasmine merely looked at Juliet until Juliet got angry.

'Mom, which do you think I should choose between going to your parents or daddy's parents?' Juliet asked her mother one afternoon.

'Sweetie, you should choose the one you want,' Juliet's mother told her.

Juliet exhaled in frustration. 'But I don't know the one to choose,' Juliet told her mother.

''Then you should just be patient; it will come to you,' Juliet's mother said.

Juliet nodded at her mother, and Juliet tried to be patient. It was one week left before vacation, and Juliet still didn't know which to choose. It felt like a weight on Juliet's shoulder, and she could not shrug it off no matter how she tried. Then it was just three days before Juliet would vacate.

'You should have your answer in three days,' Juliet's father told her. Juliet nodded.

That night, before Juliet went to bed, she made a video call with her grandfather, who was a musician, and her grandmother, who was an artist. During the call with her grandfather, Juliet learned a new song, and she sang one of her favorite songs with her grandfather. With her grandmother, Juliet showed her grandmother her recent drawing, and Juliet's grandmother examined it and praised Juliet while she also corrected Juliet on the mistakes Juliet made. Juliet had fun that night, and it made Juliet more confused as she could not choose between one of them.

'You know, you can just choose one of them, and on your next holiday, you will choose the other,' Juliet's mother told her the next day when she was eating lunch with Juliet.

'I don't want that,' Juliet said. Juliet was close to tears. Juliet did not want to miss out on the fun she could have with both of her grandparents.

On the last day that Juliet had to decide, Juliet sat in bed holding Jasmine. Jasmine was quiet as Juliet thought about the options again.

'You know Jasmine, I had fun that night when I made that video call with grandma and grandpa,' Juliet told Jasmine. Then Juliet poked Jasmine's stomach, and Jasmine blinked. Suddenly, an idea occurred to Juliet.

Juliet held Jasmine in her hands, and she danced on the bed.

'Why didn't I think about that before?' Juliet asked Jasmine, and Jasmine blinked again.

The following day, when Juliet was ready for school, Juliet's father asked her if she had made her decision.

'It's the last day of school today,' Juliet's father said.

'How long will the vacation be for?' Juliet asked her father.

'A month. That is four weeks,' Juliet's father told her.

'Dad, mom, can I go to both of your parents for vacation? I can just spend two weeks on each,' Juliet said.

Juliet's parents were surprised to see that their six-year-old girl was so intelligent.

'Sure, you can,' Juliet's parents told her.

Juliet danced, and at school that day, Juliet told Sandy, her best friend, how she had chosen the two options. Sandy said that Juliet was brilliant, and she praised Juliet's decision.

Manny's Exciting First Journey

Manny loved to see pictures of the big cities in the world. Manny would see some photos and often ask her mother which place it was. Manny enjoyed looking at views of places, hills, mountains, and oceans. Manny's mother had once asked her if she wanted to become a photographer.

'What does a photographer do?' Manny had asked. Manny was just four years old.

'A photographer takes pictures using a camera,' Manny's mother had told her.

Manny had thought about it a lot. Manny liked the idea of being the one to take those pictures that she loved gazing at. To Manny, it meant she would see those places in reality before she could capture them. It seemed like a great idea and job to Manny.

'I would become a photographer,' Manny told her mother, and Manny gave her a toothy grin. Manny's mother laughed, and she patted Manny's head.

Although Manny loved seeing pictures of places and areas, she has never been out of the city. Manny wished she could travel and see some of the places in reality, but Manny's mother was always busy and never had the time to take Manny traveling.

One day, the students were told that they would be going on an excursion to Mavina Beach. Manny was very excited. Finally, she was getting the chance to travel out of the city and to the beach too!

When Manny got home, she told her mother about it, and Manny begged her mother to pay for her to go for the excursion. Manny's mother paid, and Manny counted the days until they would go for the tour. It would be Manny's first trip out of their city to another city, and it would also be Manny's first visit to Mavina Beach.

On the day they were to go, Manny's mom took her to school in her car like she always did. Manny was so excited that she could not sit still in the car.

'I wish I could take some pictures,' Manny told her mom.

Manny's mom shook her head. Manny's mom thought that Manny was too young to handle a camera.

'When you grow older, sweetie,' Manny's mom told Manny. Manny nodded, and Manny wanted to grow up very fast.

Manny went on the excursion with her friends and her classmates. They all discussed how it would be like inside the bus. Manny looked through the window as the bus moved. Manny had never been in a bus before. She had always been taken to wherever she wanted to go in her mother's car. Manny loved the bus and the way the trees rushed past as they moved.

They got to the beach, and Manny and her mates were asked to change into their swimming suits. Manny wore her pink swimming trunk. It was Manny's favorite. Manny loved the white sand and how her feet felt in the sand. Manny was happy, and she walked around the beach.

'Do not go beyond this area,' the teachers told the pupils. The area the teacher had said was marked with a red flag.

Manny made sure that no one was looking, and she sneaked away. Manny walked past the red flag, and she looked around. Manny didn't like that the teachers had told them not to go beyond the red flag because Manny thought that the area beyond the red flag was even more beautiful. Manny wished she had a camera that she could capture with. She felt the beautiful white sand, the blue sea, and the blue sky would be lovely in a picture. She had seen pictures like that in her books before.

Manny did not look at where she was going. She was staring at the sea, and she did not notice that there was a boat in front of her. It was a huge boat. Manny collided with the boat and fell. Manny's right foot and her nose began to bleed. Manny was scared, and when she looked back, she saw that she had gone a long way from the group.

Manny began to cry. She could not walk with her leg. Manny sat in the sand and wished she had stayed with the group. It was still the same beach, after all.

After five minutes, the teachers noticed that Manny was missing, and two of them were sent out to search for her. They found Manny sitting down beside the boat, crying. Manny's leg was still bleeding, and there was blood on her face. One of the teachers carried Manny as they walked over to the group. They administered first aid to Manny.

'I'm sorry,' Manny told them. The teachers were glad that Manny realized her mistake. They gave Manny a packet of chips and a bottle of fruit drink. Manny could not play with her mates because of her leg, but she watched them while she ate her snacks. She had learned a lesson on her first trip out of the city.

The Wonderful Change in Raymond

Raymond had everything he wanted. Raymond's parents provided for him and always gave Raymond whatever he asked for. Raymond's parents worked in the same company, so they would take Raymond to school together, and they would also pick him up together. There was a part of the school where children whose parents were late to pick them usually stayed. Raymond would stay there sometimes whenever his parents were late to pick him up.

Raymond was a bad boy. He was not satisfied with what his parents gave him. Raymond would eat breakfast at home, and his mother would pack lunch and snacks for him to eat in school, but this never satisfied Raymond. Raymond would pick on the weaker ones in his class. Raymond pressured some of them to give him their food; sometimes, he pressured them to do whatever work he was assigned to in the class. Raymond would also tell them that if they reported him, he would beat them. The students would obey Raymond in fear and do as he please.

One day, Raymond's mother went to pick him in school. When Raymond entered the car, Raymond's mother noticed the toy car in his hand.

'Where did you get that from?' Raymond's mother asked.

'My friend gave me,' Raymond lied.

'Okay,' Raymond's mother said. Raymond kept on lying and making people feel bad. Raymond had no friends because his mates were scared of him and did not want to play with him.

Then a new boy came to Raymond's class. His name was Steve, and he was five years old, like Raymond. Steve was a small boy, but he had a loud voice. When Steve came, Raymond was glad because Raymond thought he had seen another prey.

During the break, Raymond asked Steve to give him his food.

'Why?' Steve asked.

Raymond was surprised. His classmates would usually do what he wanted without asking him why.

'Because I rule this place, and I want your food,' Raymond told Steve.

'That is not a good reason. I saw you eat your lunch,' Steve told Raymond.

Raymond was angry. He had never been questioned before, and he knew that if Steve defeated him, then his other classmates would never give in to him again.

'I don't care. I want your food. If you don't give me, I'll beat you,' Raymond said. Raymond expected Steve to become scared and give him his food.

Steve laughed. 'You can't beat me,' Steve said. 'My dad is a boxer, and I have known how to fight since I was a baby. You can't beat me.'

Raymond looked at Steve's red eyes, and Raymond became scared. Raymond was sure that Steve could beat him even though Steve was not big. Steve's eyes said it all.

Raymond hissed and went to meet another classmate.

'Steve, help me,' the boy that Raymond went to meet shouted. Steve defended the boy against Raymond. Steve began to protect the others from Raymond so Raymond could not bully anyone or collect their food.

After Raymond's classmates realized that Steve could defend them against Raymond, they asked Raymond to give them back all that he had collected from them. They asked for their toys, their pencils, and their books. When Raymond said he would not give them, they told him they would report him to the teachers. Raymond became scared, and he promised to give them the next day. The next day, Raymond returned the things he had collected, but some had gotten lost, and Raymond could not find them.

The owners of the lost item got angry, and they reported Raymond to the teacher. The teacher told the proprietor, and they called Raymond's parents. Raymond's parents were disappointed, and they were hurt that Raymond had been a bad boy. Raymond's parents bought new toys for Raymond's mates, and they gave Raymond's toy out to children who were less privileged.

Raymond was sad. He had no friends and no one to talk to. His classmates would not speak to him, and he had no toys to play with anymore. When Raymond could not bear it anymore, he asked his classmates in school one day to forgive him for what he had done.

Raymond's classmates forgave him, and Raymond made friends. They shared their toys with Raymond, and Raymond was no longer greedy. He had learned his lesson, and he also became friends with Steve.

Brave Branch's Journey of Freedom

Once upon a time, there was a big tree in a forest. The tree had several branches, and the branches could talk. There were six branches in all, and they had names. They were all happy, and the root was their source of food and life.

One day, the smallest branch and the last one got tired of staying with the others.

'I want to go around, travel, and see the world,' the branch said.

'You can't live without the root,' the other branches told her.

'How do you know?' the small branch asked.

'It's the way it was meant to be,' the other branches said. The small branch did not listen to them. The branch wanted to make more of its life, and it hated being on the tree all day and night long. The small branch cut itself from the tree and moved around with the wind.

The small branch was happy. The other branches watched it play and move around, and they called it to come back, but the small branch loved the adventure.

On the third day, the sun had come out fully, and it emanated its angry rays on the small branch. The small branch had nowhere to hide. The branch had also been unable to eat for three days. The branch was weary and tired. After the rays of the sun hit the branch, it began to dry up.

The small branch went back to the tree, but it was too late. The branch was already brown and drying up. It could not be fixed back to the tree, and it could not get any life from the root because it was no longer on the tree. The branch dried up entirely and died. The other branches watched with pity, but there was nothing they could do. The small branch had not survived her foolish adventure.

Caroline, the Honest Girl

Caroline has a trait that endeared everyone to her, and it was her truthfulness. Caroline's mother noticed early that Caroline never lied. Caroline told the truth even when it seemed complicated. There had been a time that Caroline's older cousin had visited them. Caroline's cousin's name was Chloe, and Chloe was a bad girl. Chloe had mistreated Caroline, and Chloe told Caroline that Caroline must not report her. When Caroline's mother returned from work, she noticed that Caroline was not happy.

'Why are you not happy? Did anything bad happen?' Caroline's mother asked.

Chloe stared hard at Caroline and expected Caroline to lie. Though Caroline was scared, Caroline could not lie.

'Chloe hit me,' Caroline told her mother. Caroline's mother got angry, and she sent Chloe back home where she came from.

Ever since then, Caroline's mother believed whatever Caroline said, and Caroline continued to be honest.

One day, Caroline was walking to school with her friend Janet when they saw a purse by the roadside.

'Look at that beautiful blue purse,' Janet said.

'So?' Caroline replied.

'We should take it,' Janet said. 'We could save money in it,' Janet chirped.

Caroline glared at Janet. 'It is not good to take what does not belong to us,' Caroline told Janet.

Janet shrugged. 'I'll take it if you don't want,' Janet said and went to take the purse. Caroline did not like what Janet was doing, but she waited for Janet to come back.

'Can't you see that it's beautiful?' Janet asked Caroline when she would come back. Janet showed the purse to Caroline, but Caroline did not touch it.

'Why does it look full?' Caroline asked. 'Is there something inside?'

Janet frowned and opened the purse. There were several dollar bills in the purse.

'Wow!' Janet said.

'It belongs to someone,' Caroline said. 'We have to give it back.'

'No!' Janet wailed. 'It belongs to me now. I found it.'

'Don't be silly. There should be a card inside the purse that will direct us to the owner,' Caroline told Janet. Janet felt sad, and she didn't budge, but Caroline snatched the purse from Janet, and Caroline searched the purse. Caroline found two Identification cards in the purse, and she was excited.

'Now, we can give it back!' Caroline said.

'No!' Janet screamed. Janet snatched the purse back from Caroline, and she also seized the ID cards from Caroline. Before Caroline could collect it back, Janet tore the cards into two pieces each, and she threw them away. Then, Janet zipped the purse and ran in the direction of the school.

Caroline was angry, but she did not run after Janet. Caroline bent on her knees, and she began to look for the ID cards that Janet had torn. Caroline found one part of the ID card in a shrub; she found another part on the sidewalk's edge. Caroline kept searching until she found the four pieces. Then Caroline stood up and went back home.

'Darling, what are you doing at home?' Caroline's mother asked when she opened the door for Caroline to enter.

Caroline showed her mother the torn cards, and she told her mother what had happened on her way to school with Janet.

'Mom, we have to return the money, right?' Caroline asked her mother.

'Yes, darling. We have to return it to the owner. What Janet is doing is called stealing,' Caroline's mother said.

Caroline nodded. 'I don't want to steal and take something that does not belong to me,' Caroline told her mother. Caroline's mother was proud of Caroline.

'We'll go to school together, and I'll tell your teacher about it,' Caroline's mother said. Caroline's mother joined the torn cards together using a sellotape.

'Will Janet get in trouble, mom?'

'No, she won't. Don't worry about it,' Caroline's mother said. Caroline's mother tidied up and followed Caroline to school. When they got to school, they went to the proprietor's office, and they reported all that happened to the proprietor. The proprietor was shocked, and he instructed a teacher to call Janet into her class. The proprietor told the teacher that Janet must come with her bag.

The teacher came back with Janet, and the proprietor searched Janet's bag. He found the blue purse in it, and when he opened the purse, he found a lot of money inside. Janet was ashamed of herself and her actions.

The proprietor was proud of Caroline, and he was embarrassed by how Janet had reacted.

'You are such an honest girl,' the proprietor said to Caroline. Caroline gave the ID cards to the proprietor, and the proprietor was shocked. The ID cards belonged to the proprietor's wife. The proprietor called his wife and asked her if she was looking for her purse. The proprietor's wife replied that she was, and the proprietor's wife rushed to the school when she heard all that had happened.

When the proprietor's wife saw the purse and saw that her money was still intact, she was grateful to Caroline. The purse had fallen off when the proprietor's wife had taken a walk in the morning.

'You are a girl of integrity,' the proprietor's wife said to Caroline.

That day, the proprietor told the other students how Caroline had displayed honesty, and Caroline was celebrated. The proprietor rewarded Caroline with gifts. Caroline's mother was happy, and Caroline was glad that she had been honest. Caroline beamed as everyone congratulated her and called her Honest Caroline.

Maria's Joyful Baby Adventure

Maria used to be the last child in the house, but now Maria's mother was having a new baby. Maria was excited. She could now have a baby sister to play with.

'What will her name be?' Maria asked her mother.

'Lily,' Maria's mother said.

'I will play with Lily,' Maria told Daisy, her older sister.

'I will play with her too,' Daisy said.

Maria nodded. 'We will both play with her, and she will be our baby.'

Daisy and Maria looked forward to the arrival of their baby sister. Maria was five years old while Daisy was seven years old.

'When will Lily come?' Maria asked her mother.

'Very soon,' Maria's mother told them.

One morning, when Maria's mother woke up, she had lost the baby. Maria's father and mother told Maria and Daisy about losing the baby. They were all sad. They had wanted to see Lily, and they had all anticipated her birth. Maria cried while her mother consoled her. There was nothing they could do about it.

After a while, Maria's mother began to have a big stomach again.

'Will the baby come now?' Maria asked.

'Yes,' Maria's mother said, but she was not sure. Maria and Daisy prayed that the baby would come this time.

'Will she still be Lily?' Maria asked her father.

'No,' Maria's father said.

'Why? She should still be Lily!' Maria wailed.

'Okay. We will name her Lily,' Maria's mother and father said. Maria was half happy. Maria felt that she would be totally happy when Lily was born.

The day that Lily was to be born, it was a Saturday, and Maria and Lily were at home with their parents. Maria's mother began to groan. It scared Maria.

'What is happening to mommy?' Maria asked.

'Lily says she's coming today,' Maria's father told her. They all went to the hospital, but Maria's mother went in alone with the doctors. Maria, Daisy, and their father waited outside. They waited a long time before the doctor came to tell them that they could see the new baby. Maria, Daisy, and their father went in to see Maria's mother and the baby.

'She looks like me!' Maria exclaimed when she saw the baby. Everyone agreed that Lily looked like Maria. When they went home, everyone called the baby Lily, but Maria called Lily Maria's baby. Maria was thrilled. Lily had taken a long time to come, but Maria felt that it was worth it. She now had her baby to play with.

Mira's Magical Bond with Her Twin

Mira and Mia were identical twins. Their parents were Mr. and Mrs. Lucas. Mira and Mia looked so much alike that even their parents found it challenging to differentiate them. They were of the same height; weight and they wore the same dresses.

Mira was a good girl while Mia was a bad girl, but whenever Mia did something terrible, she would lie that it was Mira that did it. One day, Mia took her mother's lipstick to school and broke it. Mira had warned Mia not to take the lipstick, but Mia did not listen. Then Mia returned it to her mother's room and pretended that nothing happened. When Mrs. Lucas saw it, she was shocked.

'Who broke my lipstick?' Mrs. Lucas asked.

'It was Mira,' Mia lied.

'It was Mia,' Mira said.

Mrs. Lucas did not know who to believe, so she left them alone. Another day, Mrs. Lucas walked into Mira and Mia's room with a stern look.

'Who is Mia?' Mrs. Lucas asked because she could not tell by herself. The twins looked alike.

Mira pointed to Mia, and Mia pointed to Mira.

'You are Mia!' Mira shouted.

'Stop lying! You are Mia!' Mia shouted also. Mia was very convinced with her act that Mrs. Lucas thought Mira was Mia. Mrs. Lucas took Mira to her room and punished her because the proprietor had called to say that Mia was causing trouble in school. Mia did not feel bad that Mira had been punished for what she did. Mia went on with her nasty ways, and many times, it was Mira who suffered for it.

'I don't like how you act,' Mira told Mia one day. Mira was crying. She was tired of being punished for her sister's offenses.

'How is it my fault that they can't recognize me?' Mia asked.

'Stop pushing the blame on me!' Mira exclaimed. 'I don't like being punished unjustly.'

'Sorry,' Mia said, but Mia did not stop. She continued misbehaving and letting Mira pay for it.

Eventually, Mira became tired of the situation. Mira thought of what she would do, and she came up with a plan. One night, while Mia was fast asleep, Mira went to her parents' bedroom. Mira knocked, and her parents invited her in. Mr. and Mrs. Lucas were shocked to see that one of their daughters was still awake.

'Who are you, and what is wrong?' they asked her.

'I am Mira,' Mira told them, and Mira explained what had been happening and how Mia had made her pay for her offenses. Mr. and Mrs. Lucas found it difficult to believe.

'How do we know it's not you who has been misbehaving and you want to throw it on Mia because Mia had always made sure of your punishment?' Mr. Lucas asked.

Mira felt sad, but she understood her parents' disbelief. 'Those wrongdoings I was punished for were done by Mia, not me.'

Mira's parents found it difficult to believe one side of the story.

'Okay, I have a plan,' Mira told them. Mira asked her parents to place a tiny mark on her hand and recognize her as Mira. Then, Mira asked them to come to her and Mia's room very early in the morning when they were still asleep, and Mr. and Mrs. Lucas should call her and Mia's name.

'Anyone that answers to the name you call is the owner of the name, and then you can look at the mark and know that I am telling the truth,' Mira said. Mr. and Mrs. Luca agreed, and they made a mark on Mira's arm with a permanent marker. Mira left their room and went back to her room.

Early in the morning, Mr. and Mrs. Lucas sneaked into Mia and Mira's room. Mira and Mia were still fast asleep.

'Mia!!!' Mr. and Mrs. Lucas shouted at the same time. Mia woke up suddenly and answered. Mrs. Lucas held Mia and checked her hand. There was no mark on it. Mr. and Mrs. Lucas called Mira, and when Mira woke up, they found the little mark on her hand. Then, Mr. and Mrs. Lucas realized that Mira had been telling the truth and that Mia had acted wrongly towards her sister. Mr. and Mrs. Lucas wrote the names of each twin on the twin's hand, and they made Mia apologize to Mira.

From that day, Mia could not blame Mira for whatever she did, and she could not disguise she was Mira. Mia turned a new leaf and changed her bad manners.

The Lion's Majestic Rule Over the Elephant

A long time ago, in the jungle, the animals said that they wanted a king to rule over them. It was such a great idea that they decided to choose who would be the king that would lead them.

'I can be king,' Tortoise said.

'You are unfit!' the other animals retorted.

'I could be king,' snail said. The animal laughed.

'You are not even worthy of a throne,' they had said. All the small animals like rabbits, hare, chickens, birds also said they wanted to be king, but they were too small, and they were not chosen.

'The king should be an animal that is huge and wise,' the animals decided. They asked themselves who would fit such a classification.

'That would be me,' Lion said.

'Or perhaps me,' Elephant said.

The animals became thoughtful. The Lion and Elephant were two animals that were respected in the jungle.

'The two of you have to take a test,' the animals said.

'What kind of test?' the Lion and the Elephant asked.

'A fighting test to prove your prowess,' the animals said. 'We will have it on the next market day.'

Lion and Elephant started preparing for the fight, and the two of them were seen performing exercises in their houses. When the market day came, all the animals gathered at the market square. Everyone wanted to witness the fight by themselves. A large square stage had been constructed, and Lion and the Elephant were asked to step into it.

Lion and Elephant stared at one another menacingly until the whistle was blown. The race had begun! Elephant charged at Lion immediately, but Lion was expecting that, and the Lion stepped out of Elephant's way. Elephant was huge, so it was too late to stop, and Elephant hit his head on the strong concrete that was constructed around the stage. Elephant hit the wall and collapsed immediately. Blood started flowing, and because the Elephant was too big, he could not stand up. The other animals helped Elephant to stand up and dragged him from the stage.

Lion won the battle, and he was made the king of the jungle. The animals realized that mightiness was needed to be king, but flexibility was more important. From thereon, the Lion came to be known as the king of the jungle, and he was also king over the huge Elephant.

Smiling Sun's Bright Adventure

There was peace on earth at the time. It was so calm on earth that the man of the sky would sometimes go to sleep because he trusted the people on earth, and he knew that they would not cause trouble. Everyone loved one another and assisted one another during difficulties.

The sun used to smile on the world at that time. The rays of the sun were not harsh, and a person could stand under the sun for a day and not sweat. The moon was also cool. People loved day and night, and it was difficult for people to say they preferred day or night. Animals and humans were happy. People were free to do as they pleased, and they always did the right thing. Doing the right thing came easy to everyone. It was a beautiful world.

Suddenly, people got tired of living like that. Some of them wanted more wealth and stopped rendering help. They resorted to stealing and kidnapping, and a lot of other vices came to the world. There was no longer peace, and people lived in fear of one another. It was dangerous to walk in the day, and night was worse. Parents locked their children indoors at night, and adults were wary of walking the streets at night. There was bloodshed, and people did not get tired of doing evil. The good people on earth were not many.

The man in the sky woke up one day and noticed that everything had gone wrong. He tried to help, but it was too late. Then the man of the sky decided to leave the people in the world alone to act as they wanted. It was their business, he said.

The people got worse, and every non-living thing was affected. The ocean got angry and started swallowing people. The sun stopped smiling, and it would stare harshly at the people, shining its harsh rays on them. The nights were dark and cold, and the day was hot and exhausting, yet the people did not change.

One day, in a house, a girl was born. She was named Sheila. Sheila grew up, and when Sheila could talk, she learned about how the world used to be happy and peaceful. Sheila was surprised that the world used to be like that because all that Sheila knew since she was born was chaos and battle.

'Why did it change?' Sheila asked her grandmother who had told her the story.

'People became tired of love,' Sheila's grandma said. 'They became greedy.'

'Is there no way out?' Sheila asked. Sheila felt that it would be great to go back to those days when everything was calm; she wanted to go back to when people could sit outside at night and stare up at the moon. Sheila felt that it would be cool to return to the time when the sun smiled, and the ocean cared.

'I don't know if the world can we be saved,' Sheila's grandma said.

'I want to save the world,' Sheila said.

Sheila's grandmother laughed. She thought that Sheila was joking.

After hearing the story, Sheila began to look for ways to save the world and bring back the lost times.

'Do you know that the sun used to smile?' Sheila asked her age grades.

'No,' some of them would say, and Sheila would tell them the history that her grandma told them. Most of them did not care.

'As long as I'm safe, it's not my business, some of them said.'

'That's mean. Why would you say that?' Sheila would ask.

'That is what my father said,' one of Sheila's friends said.

'That's the cause of the trouble in the world. People are just too selfish and care about themselves alone,' Sheila would inform them.

Sheila lectured many of her mates, and several of them loved the idea of going back to the past. Sheila was their leader, and she taught them and motivated them.

'But how do we make everything be like before?' A boy asked. His name was Caleb.

'I'm still thinking about it,' Sheila said. Then an idea came to Sheila one day.

'We can all call on the man in the sky with a selfless heart. Nobody who is selfish is allowed to go with us. We will shout until the man in the sky hears and tell him to bring back the old times. What do you think?' Sheila asked them.

The others thought it was a good idea, and they set to work. They were to act on their idea the next day. Many of the children in various houses went out that afternoon.

'You are going to be burnt from the rays of the sun,' Sheila told them. Some of them did not want to get burnt, so they walked away. Sheila was glad. She only wanted selfless people with her. They began to chant under the harsh sunlight.

Man in the sky, see us!

Man in the sky, we've come!

Bring back old times

Bring back our peace

Take the selfish ones away

Let it end

Oh, Sun! Smile. We want to see your smile.

Bring back old times

Oh, Ocean! Care. We want you to play with us and not swallow us.

Man of the sky, we've come.

Let peace reign.

They chanted like this for a week. Sheila and her friends did not get tired. Their skin was getting tanned, but they were selfless. They were ready to give their lives for a better world.

On the last day of the week, the man in the sky saw the perseverance of Sheila and her friends, and he granted their request. Immediately, the ocean stopped roaring and calmed. The sun smiled, and Sheila and her friends danced in triumph.

People who were selfishly working noticed that the heat of the day reduced, and they were surprised. Suddenly, the people that were outside in the sun shouted.

'The sun is smiling again!' they shouted.

The greedy people were surprised, and when they went outside, they saw it was true, and they also saw Sheila and her friends dancing. They all became ashamed that it was their fault the world was being destroyed previously. They apologized to the good people, and they changed.

The world became a better place again. The sun smiled, and the moon was once again cool. Children could stay outside until late at night, and the world was beautiful once again. Sheila and her friends were glad to be a part of it.

The Curious Trio's Learning Adventure

Linda, Grace, and Beth were close friends. They lived on the same street and attended the same school. The friends all had a passion for studying, and in school, when their mates when playing, Linda, Grace, and Beth would be reading and quizzing themselves on what they read.

The friends also cared about one another, and they would share their food and snacks together. People in school knew that the three of them were close friends, and they avoided getting any of them angry; because if Linda were offended, Grace and Beth would also be offended. The friends' motto was, Studying Pays.

One day, a spelling competition was brought to their school. Beth, Linda, and Grace were elated. It was a test of their abilities. The three friends registered for the competition, and they studied exceptionally well for it.

Although there was a combined lesson in school for the competition, Linda, Beth, and Grace did not let their training end there. Sometimes, they would go to Linda's house because she had many learning materials, and they would be there all day learning new words and their meanings.

'What is mutual trust among people?' Beth would ask.

'Ca-ma-ra-de-rie,' Linda would reply. Then someone else would ask another question, and another would reply. They often took breaks while studying to watch cartoons, but they had a drafted schedule, and they stuck to it.

Linda, Beth, and Grace's parents would watch their children, and they would be proud of who they were. The teachers also liked how the three friends were serious with their academics.

Then the day of the spelling competition arrived. Linda woke up with a severe headache, and she was shaking all over.

'You have a fever. You can't go to school,' Linda's mother said.

'But I have to be at the competition,' Linda said.

Linda's mother refused, but Linda was adamant that she would go, so Linda's mother had to give in. Linda was taken to the hospital quickly before the time that she would go for the competition. Linda was given some drugs before her mother drove her to the hall where the competition would hold.

'What is wrong?' Beth and Grace asked when they saw Linda.

'I have a fever,' Linda replied. Beth and Grace said that Linda should have stayed at home, but Linda refused. They practiced some more before it was time for the competition.

Linda, Grace, and Beth were representing their school in the junior category. The three of them were called out, and they competed against another school. The candidates of the other school were a boy and two girls.

'We will win,' Linda told her friends, and the competition started.

It was ten questions, and on the ninth question, Linda's team was leading with six. As the last question was asked, Linda answered it and fainted.

Everyone was shocked. Linda's parents ran to the stage, and Linda was taken to the hospital. Beth and Grace were worried, but they were not allowed to leave the hall. After the commotion ended, the winners were announced, and it was Beth, Linda, and Grace that won. Beth and Grace were awarded, and they rushed to the hospital afterward.

'Did we win?' Linda asked them. Linda was lying on the hospital bed, looking weak.

'Yes, we did!' Beth and Grace exclaimed.

Linda was excited and glad that she had participated in the competition before she fainted.

'Studying pays,' the three friends said, and they smiled.

The Mystery of the Dangerous Snakes

Once upon a time, humans and animals lived together. In those days, snakes were kept as pets, and humans loved snakes because they were loyal animals. They hung the snakes on their neck whenever they went out, and the snakes never bit them.

The snakes would move around the house of their owners, and they would help with little chores in the house like passing paper and pen from one person to another or passing a note. Sometimes, snakes would fold themselves around a cup and give it to whoever needed it. The only thing the snake could not do was talk, and they could not walk also.

In one house, William had a big snake. William fed his snake as frequently as he could manage. William gave the snake breakfast, lunch, and dinner, and William's snake was happy.

One day, William went out, and he left his child at home with his wife. William expected to return home that day, but something came up, and Williams could not go back home. After two days, Williams went home, and Williams was shocked to see that his wife and his son were dead. The snake had gotten hungry, but William's wife had not known. Then, the snake bit William's wife and William's child. William was hurt, and then he got angry. Williams took a rod, and he tried to kill the snake. William pursued the snake around the house, but he could not catch it as the snake crawled away quickly.

The snake managed to crawl out of the house, and William followed it. William ran after it until he caught up with it, and William hit the snake's head with the big wood he carried. William hit the snake continuously until the snake died.

Other snakes in other houses saw as William killed the snake, and they also got angry. They attacked the humans that owned them, and humans and serpents began to fight. It was a real battle because every house had a snake. They fought and tried to kill the snakes that they had. Some humans and snakes got injured, but some snakes managed to crawl away into the forest.

Since then, the snake has become a wild animal, never to be kept as a pet again. Also, whenever a snake sees a human, the snake's first thought is usually to strike the human down.

Amazing Story of How Dogs Became Our Pets

Dogs used to be a wild animal in the past. The dog was like the Lion, leopard, and tiger, and it was dangerous. Dogs also lived in the forest.

One day, there was a commotion in the village. It was dark at night, and a dog jumped the village's fence and ran into it. The villagers were unprepared, so they were scared that the dog would kill them. One man quickly got his gun, and he was about to shoot the dog when the dog talked.

'No, don't shoot me. I am here to help,' the dog said.

The man did not shoot. They took the dog into a house, and the dog told them that the wild animals were planning to wage war against the village. The wild animals planned to enter the village and destroy everyone in it. The dog told the people that he did not support the plan, so he had revealed the plan to them. The people were grateful, and they asked the dog to stay and live with them. The dog disagreed.

'I don't want them to suspect anything. I have to go back now,' the dog told the people.

The people wished that the dog could stay, but they agreed that it was better for the dog to return. The dog left the village and returned to the forest.

The villagers started preparing for the war that the wild animals were planning. The villagers trained themselves day and night. They got their guns ready and sharpened their cutlasses.

On the day that the wild animals were to come to the village, the villagers were expecting them. Packs of lions, tigers, and leopards ran into the town, ready to devour the people, but the people were ready. They shot at the wild animals, and they cut at the ones they were unable to attack. It was a long fight because the animals were vicious, but the villagers finally won after killing all the wild animals. After this, the dog emerged, and the villagers were grateful to him. They begged the dog to live with them, and the dog agreed. The dog started living with humans from that day, and until now, dogs keep showing loyalty to humans.

The Adventure of the House Thief

There has been trouble in the house of Mr. and Mrs. Robinson. Things were missing, but no one knew how or who was taking them. Five people lived in the house. There was Mr. Robinson, Mrs. Robinson, their two children, Tim and Sidney, and their housekeeper, Kimberly. Kimberly was an aged woman, so Mr. and Mrs. Robinson counted her out of the robbery. They felt that Kimberly was an honest and loyal employee, and she was also old, so she could not steal from them. Something went missing in the house every week, and this annoyed Mr. and Mrs. Robinson.

'Who took my newly bought pearl necklace?' Mrs. Robinson shouted from her room one day. Mrs. Robinson was preparing for a party, and she was already dressed. All that Mrs. Robinson needed was her pearl necklace, and she would go, but she could not find it. Mrs. Robinson marched to their living room, and she found Tim and Sidney watching a movie there.

'Did any of you take my newly bought pearl necklace?' Mrs. Robinson asked.

'No, mother,' Tim and Sidney replied.

'But I can't find it,' Mrs. Robinson said.

'It should be in your room, mom,' Sidney said.

'Mom, you know that we never go to your room without your permission. We didn't see your necklace,' Tim said. Tim and Sidney concentrated on their TV show. Mrs. Robinson felt tired. She did not know what to do, but she wore another necklace, and she went to the party.

When Mrs. Robinson returned from the party, her husband had also returned from work. Mrs. Robinson told him of the recent development of her missing pearl necklace. It got Mr. Robinson worried.

'You don't think this could be the children's work, do you?'

Mrs. Robinson frowned. She trusted her children, but she also knew that things do not just disappear. It had just started one day, and she had lost ten necklaces, bracelets, rings, and some of them were made of gold.

'Perhaps, it's time to suspect Kimberly,' Mrs. Robinson said, but Mr. Robinson shook his head.

'Kimberly would not do such a thing!' Mr. Robinson said.

'Tim and Sidney would never do this too. Sidney is just six while Tim is ten,' Mrs. Robinson said.

'Then who did?' Mr. Robinson asked.

'It remains only the two of us,' Mrs. Robinson said, but she knew that Mr. Robinson was not the thief. Mr. Robinson had also lost three of his gold wristwatches.

'We should call the police,' Mrs. Robinson said, and Mr. Robinson nodded.

They called the police, and the police officer asked many questions. Mr. and Mrs. Robinson explained that there were just five of them in the house, and none could have stolen the items. They also told the police officer that the items were being stolen only in their room. No one else complained about theft in the house. It was only in Mr. and Mrs. Robinson's bedroom that things went missing.

The police officer was a smart man, but he was also confused.

'You say that no other person has access to your room, except your little children?' The police officer asked.

'Yes,' Mr. and Mrs. Robinson said.

The police officer thought about it for a while. Then his face brightened as he got an idea, and he told Mr. and Mrs. Robinson about it. The officer told Mr. and Mrs. Robinson to empty their room of all furniture and search thoroughly for the missing items. Mr. and Mrs. Robinson didn't like the idea, but they agreed to do it. The police officer was glad, and he left.

Mr. and Mrs. Robinson called some movers, and they helped them move their furniture out of the room. When the movers took out the bed, all the missing accessories were found on the floor where the bed used to be. A rat was lying on the floor next to the accessories. Mr. and Mrs. Robinson were shocked. Tim and Sidney kept laughing. They thought it was funny. None of them could have guessed that a rat was the thief that was troubling them in the house. When the rat saw them, he ran through their feet and out the door, and he never came back again.

Mr. and Mrs. Robinson were glad that they had taken the police officer's advice. The house went back to normal after the thief had left.

Magical Quest of Roland and His Wand

Roland lived with his parents on Saint Monica's Street. Roland's parents worked in the afternoons and got home at night. The only time Roland saw his parents were in the morning and the night, except during weekends and holidays.

Roland's parents got him a nanny, and they also bought Roland many toys, cartoons, and books. Roland liked having all those things, but Roland was five years old, and he felt lonely being by himself every time. Roland played with his mates in school, but he would be by himself at home whenever he left school. Roland's nanny was old, so Roland could not play with her. Roland would often wish that he had a sister or a brother to play with. Roland often felt lonely and sad.

One day, while Roland was sitting by himself in the playground, he saw something in the sand. Roland went to the spot, and he took out the object from the sand. Roland saw that it was a wand, and Roland was surprised to find a wand in the sand. Roland had a couple of toy wands at home, but the one he saw looked different. It was not made of wood, plastic, or metal like the ones Roland had at home, and the wand in the sand was also shining. Roland took the wand and slipped it into his pocket. Roland wondered if it belonged to anyone in his class or if a fairy had mistakenly dropped it while performing her magic. Roland decided that if anyone were looking for the wand, he would return it. Roland took the wand to school and back home that week, but no one was looking for it.

After one week, Roland felt that it was a magic wand, and Roland was happy. He thought about what he would wish for. Roland decided he would lock himself in his room after school, and he would make a wish.

After Roland got home, he locked his room. Roland took out the wand, and he made a wish.

'Oh, magic wand. Let my parents always be with me,' Roland wished, and he waved the wand. The wand released a colorful smoke, and Roland knew that it was real.

The next day, Roland's parents did not go out. They both got a job online, and they did not have to go to work again. Roland was excited. Whenever he came back from school, his parents would be at home. He could talk with his dad and play with his mom. Roland kept the wand safe.

After a while, Roland wanted more than his parents to stay at home. Roland wanted a younger sibling. So, one afternoon while Roland's parents were working, he locked himself in his room, and he wished to have a younger sibling. Roland's mother's stomach started to get big.

'Mom, why is your stomach getting big?' Roland asked.

'You are going to have a younger brother,' Roland's mother told him.

'Really?' Roland asked.

'Yes,' Roland's mother said, and Roland did a happy dance. His second wish had worked. Roland's mother's stomach grew bigger, and Roland was pleased. He was getting everything that he wanted.

One afternoon, while Roland was playing with his toys in his room, he took the wand and stared at it. He mistakenly shook it, and three fairies appeared in his room. Roland was scared.

'Do not fear,' the fairies said. They were colorful fairies of blue, red, and yellow.

'You have just used your last wish, and we have come to collect the wand,' the fairies told Roland. Roland felt sad that he had wasted his third wish, but he gave the fairies the wand, and he thanked them. The fairies disappeared with the wand.

Roland was happy that his family was together, and he would have a brother. The wand had helped him, and Roland was no longer a lonely and sad boy.

Abigail's Musical Journey with the Fairy's Grant

Abigail loved music, and she loved singing more, but Abigail had a bad voice. Whenever Abigail opened her mouth to sing, people would tell her to keep silent or stop singing because she had a terrible voice. It was also like that in school. Even Abigail's best friend, Dess, could not bear Abigail's voice.

'You have a good talking voice, but it's not good for singing,' Dess would tell Abigail. This made Abigail sad because Abigail loved singing, and she wanted to become a singer.

When Abigail complained to her mother that she did not have a good singing voice, Abigail's mother told Abigail that it was not important.

'You can do something else,' Abigail's mother told her.

'But I want to become a singer!' Abigail wailed.

'Don't worry about it. Your voice can become better,' Abigail's mother said. Abigail felt miserable. She wanted to sing and sing beautifully so that everyone would love to hear her sing.

Abigail would stare out her window after her parents had kissed her goodnight. She would stare at the moon and practice singing. Abigail would sing and wish in her mind that her voice was good.

One night, Abigail said her wish out loud.

'I wish that my voice was good,' Abigail said.

'Okay. Why do you want that?' a voice said. The beautiful voice scared Abigail, and she moved away from her open window. A pink fairy flew into Abigail's room. Abigail's mouth felt open, and Abigail touched her face with her cool palms. That was what Abigail usually did when she wanted to check if she was not dreaming.

'It's a fairy,' Abigail said.

The fairy laughed at what Abigail said. 'Yes, I'm a fairy. You can call me Gail,' the fairy said.

'Girl?' Abigail asked. It seemed weird to name someone a girl. It was like calling a child, boy, Abigail thought.

'No,' the fairy said. 'I'm Abigail but known as Gail.'

'Wow. I am Abigail too!' Abigail said.

'Really?' the fairy asked. The fairy was happy, and she flew and danced around Abigail's room. 'I'm so happy,' the fairy said.

Abigail laughed. She was happy too that a fairy had the same name as her.'

'I will happily grant your wish,' the fairy told Abigail.

'You grant wishes?' Abigail asked. The fairy nodded, and Abigail quickly sat on the bed and told the fairy her wish again. The fairy asked Abigail why she wanted a good voice, and Abigail told the fairy that she wanted to become a singer.

'I'm a singer too,' the fairy said. Abigail was glad that the fairy understood her. No one had understood Abigail before. The fairy waved her wand and said some magic words. Abigail's wish was granted.

'Sing a song,' the fairy urged Abigail.

Abigail sang.

> *Power dwells in me,*
> *I can do and undo,*
> *I am strong,*
> *I can change the world,*
> *I am the future of the world.*

It was Abigail's favorite song, and as she sang it, Abigail could hear her voice sounded better. The fairy's magic had worked. Abigail felt very happy that she started crying. Now, she could be a singer as she has always wanted. The fairy told Abigail not to cry, and they both sang together, and their voices were melodious. When it was almost midnight, the fairy told Abigail that she had to go. The fairy promised Abigail that she would visit Abigail often, and Abigail was glad. Abigail slept, and there was a big smile on her face as she dreamed of fairies and beautiful lands.

Abigail's mother came to wake her for school the following day, but Abigail was already awake and singing. Abigail's mother was surprised.

'Your voice sounds different,' she told Abigail.

'Yes,' Abigail said and smiled. Abigail quickly prepared for school. She was excited about her excellent voice, and she wanted to sing for her friends in school.

When Abigail sang in school, everyone was surprised. Abigail's voice had changed.

'You would make a great singer,' Dess told Abigail. Abigail smiled as she sang, and people loved it. It was her only wish to sing, and she was glad that she had wished it so much and she had gotten it. Abigail knew that she would make a great singer.

Lazy Boy's Surprising Lesson from the Hardworking Girl!

There was once a boy called Albert and a girl named Beatrice. Beatrice and Albert lived next to one another and attended the same school, but they were completely different. Beatrice was hardworking while Albert was lazy. Beatrice would wake up when her mother woke her up, but Albert was not like that. Albert was lazy in everything, and he would take a long time to get ready for school. Albert and Beatrice's parents wanted them to walk to school together and walk back together, but Albert usually delayed, so Beatrice usually ended up leaving him. Albert would dawdle, and he was also lazy in doing his homework.

Albert and Beatrice continued like this; none of them changed. Beatrice did not transform to bad, and Albert did not transform too good.

Then it was time for promotional examination, and their ability in the exam would determine if they would move to the next class.

'Let us read and prepare together,' Beatrice told Albert in school one day. Albert agreed.

Beatrice went to Albert's house the next day.

'I'm tired. I don't have the time,' Albert told Beatrice. Albert was always too tired to study, so Beatrice studied alone until it was time for the examinations.

On the day of the examination, Beatrice was prepared, but Albert was not. Albert came up with examination fever. They wrote their exams, and when the result came out, Beatrice passed, and Albert failed.

Beatrice was excited. Her hard work and relentless study had paid off. All Albert did was cry. He was ashamed of himself. Albert was the last in the class. Albert wished that he had studied when Beatrice called him. Albert wished that he had not been lazy, but it was too late for him.

Alex on the Exciting Quest to Tame a Hyena

Alex was going on an excursion to his school. It was a trip to the Wild of Lora. The Wild of Lora was a famous wildlife park in the city, and Alex was excited to be going. Alex had wanted to go in the past, but his parents never got the chance to take him. Alex paid for the trip, and he waited impatiently for the day they would go.

On the said day, Alex's father drove him to school, and Alex was enthusiastic as he joined the students in the school bus. They got to the park safely, and they met other people and tourists there. The park ranger led Alex's school team through the park. Alex loved the garden. As they moved through the park, Alex saw several wild animals, and he was fascinated. Alex wished he could get closer to them and touch them, but the teachers had warned them that the animals were dangerous.

Soon, they got to a cage with a hyena in it. The hyena was hitting its head against the iron cage desperately. Everyone was shocked, including the park ranger. The park ranger tried to appease the hyena, but the animal was not listening. The animal seemed angry about something. Alex felt that he had the chance to render help.

'It's okay, shush,' Alex said. All eyes turned to him, and they wondered what he was doing.

'Shush,' Alex told the hyena again. Alex stretched out his hands and stood in front of the hyena's cage. The hyena stopped hitting his head, and he kept staring at Alex in curiosity. The park ranger and the other students were impressed with what Alex had done. Alex was rewarded with gifts when they left the park.

The Tale of the First Son

A long time ago, there lived a family. They were known as the Scotts. The family comprises six people, Mr. and Mrs. Scott, Dave, Helen, Becca, and Simon. Dave's parents were wealthy, and they provided whatever he needed for him and his siblings. Dave had two sisters and a brother. Dave's sisters are Helen and Becca, while Dave's brother is Simon. Dave was the oldest child in the family. Dave lived anyhow he wanted, and he lavished money however he wanted because his parents were wealthy. Dave believed he would inherit all that his father had someday, so Dave felt he did not have to work.

Dave had a lot of friends who did not care about him. They only wanted to spend out of Dave's money, but Dave did not know.

Dave's parents warned him about his lifestyle, but Dave would tell them to leave him alone, and Dave's siblings were ashamed of how Dave lived. They tried talking to their brother also, but Dave never listened.

One day, Mr. Scott fell sick. It was a severe illness, and they feared that he would die. They took him to the best hospitals, but Mr. Scott did not get well. His condition worsened until he died. Everyone was sad. Mr. Scott had been loved by all, and he had helped a lot of people.

After the funeral, the lawyer went to Scott's house to reveal Mr. Scott's will to them. Dave was sad about his father's death, but he knew that his share of the will would be great, so that made him happy. The lawyer showed them the testament that Mr. Scott had given. Mr. Scott had given the same percentage of his property to his four children, he had granted a higher rate to his wife, and the rest he had given to charity. The Scotts were happy about the arrangement.

Although Dave was expecting more, he was content with what he had been given. Dave left home despite his family's plea to stay and invest his share of his father's will properly. Dave withdrew his share, and he got an apartment. Dave started treating his friends to his money. He gave them expensive accessories and hosted parties. Dave was not working, but he was spending a lot. In less than a year, Dave ran out of money. It came as a shock to Dave. There was no money at all, and he had nothing to rely on. When Dave's friends realized that he no longer had money, they abandoned him. Dave had no one to rely on. He was penniless, and he had no food to eat.

Dave went back home to his mother and siblings. Dave's siblings had invested their share of their money well, and it was paying off for them. Dave felt embarrassed to ask for money because they had been given the same share, but Dave's family accepted him and gave him money again.

Dave was humbled, and when he collected the money, he invested it well. Dave built an online marketplace for people to trade, and it became a big platform. Dave made a lot of money, and he became rich again, but this time, Dave did not waste the money. Dave did not buy flashy things, and he stayed humble. This way, the wrong friends did not come back into Dave's life. Dave's kept working and making his family proud.

Join Cordelia on Her Determined Quest

Cordelia was a colored girl who was admitted into a huge school. Cordelia got to the school through her determination. It was one of the best schools in the city. Cordelia was excited to have gotten into the school.

When Cordelia resumed school, she realized that she was the only colored girl. Cordelia felt strange. Some people would stare at Cordelia for a long time, and some people would point at her. Cordelia did not like it, but she endured, and she continued learning in the school. Cordelia also wished that another person of color would come to the school.

In Cordelia's third month at the school, another colored girl was admitted, and Cordelia was glad. Cordelia met the girl whose name was Tabitha. They both decided to start a movement. They spread the news among coloreds like them about attending the school. They felt it was wrong that there were few colors in the school. Cordelia and Tabitha did their campaign off the school grounds.

After a while, their efforts began to pay off. Coloreds began to apply to the school. Many of them were brilliant, so they were chosen. Cordelia and Tabitha were glad. They pushed on. They wanted as many whites as coloreds in the school.

After their goal was accomplished, Cordelia and Tabitha were glad. It had taken time and energy, but they succeeded because they were determined.

The Amazing Adventure of Obeying School Rules

There were three boys who went to the same school. Their names were Jake, Sam, and Robert. The three boys were disobedient in their classes at home, and they bullied younger students also. The school had caught them disobeying school rules many times, and they had been punished, but they did not stop. They continued violating, and the school continued punishing them.

One of the offenses the three boys usually commit is that they snake away from the school during school hours. The school was a boarding school located in a riverine area, and the school directors usually told them not to go out of the school without permission. Sam and his friends often sneak out of the school, though. They did not care about the school rules.

'The rules are too rigid,' Sam had said in class one day. It had gotten different responses from the students. Many of the students thought that the rules were meant to keep them safe. Sam did not like it. He called those people who defended the rules weak. Sam was mean and cruel, and he continued disobeying the rules with his friends.

One day, Sam, Jake, and Robert sneaked out of the school like they used to. There was a stream that was a distance away from the school. The three boys decided to go there to play. They had left school while class was going on. The three of them thought that the lesson was boring, so they left.

'We can even try to fish,' Jake said when they got close to the stream. The other two agreed.

The stream was small, and shrubs were surrounding it. The boys had been there many times before.

They sat on the small bushes that surrounded the stream. Sam and Jake tried to catch little fish in the stream with their hands. They did not take fishing items with them, and they were unable to catch the fish. Robert lay on his back and stared at the dull sky.

'Look at that cloud,' Robert said. Jake and Sam went to Robert, and they looked at the sky. The cloud looked like a man driving a motorcycle. The three boys laughed. They felt it was more fun out there than in the school. They all laid on their backs and watched the clouds.

'Ouch,' Sam suddenly screamed. Sam, Jake, and Robert stood up immediately. They saw a snake crawling away. The snake had bitten Sam. Sam fell and started crying. He was in so much pain. Jake and Robert did not know what to do. Jake remembered what he had learned in health education about when someone had a snake bite. Jake took off his shirt, and he tied it around Sam's leg. Then, Jake and Robert carried Sam to school. When they got to school, Sam was already unconscious.

Sam was rushed to the hospital while Jake and Robert were asked to narrate what had happened. After Jake and Robert narrated it, the proprietor was shocked and disappointed in them. He called an assembly of all the students. The proprietor told the students what Jake, Sam, and Robert had done.

It was disgracing. The proprietor expelled Sam, Jake, and Robert from the school.

It took a while before Sam got well, but when he did, he could not go to the school because he had been expelled. The three boys learned the hard way that rules were meant to keep them safe.

Marcus and the Magical Wishing Well

Marcus was a six-year-old boy who lived with his father, stepmother, and stepbrother. Marcus's mother died when Marcus was still a baby, and Marcus's father had married another wife. Marcus's stepmother did not like him, and she mistreated him. She also made her son Liam dislike Marcus, and many times, Liam would beat Marcus though Liam was five years old. Marcus felt miserable, and he would always cry, but Marcus's father was not always around. Marcus's father did not know what was happening with Marcus. Whenever Marcus's father was around, Marcus's stepmother would treat him well, and she would act caring towards him.

The way Marcus was being treated at home affected his academics. Marcus failed woefully in his schoolworks, but this didn't bother Marcus's stepmother. She was unconcerned for Marcus.

One day, after school, Marcus did not go home. He knew that he would be subjected to insults and beatings, so he walked around. As Marcus strolled the streets, he came to a well. There was a tag on the well that said, Wishing Well. Marcus had a coin that his father had given him earlier that week. Marcus had kept it for the day his stepmother would not give him food, and he might need it. Marcus took the coin out of his bag and threw it in the well.

'I wish I could be happy,' Marcus said. Nothing happened, and Marcus felt terrible. Marcus had thought that there would be a poof or a breeze, but there was nothing. Marcus left the well and walked around some more. When Marcus got ready to go home, he passed by the spot where the well was again, but there was not well there. Marcus ran to the area and looked around, but there was not well. Marcus did not know what to think. All he knew was that his coin was gone, and when he got home, his stepmother would punish him for being late.

When Marcus got home, the house was disorganized, and the doors and windows were thrown open. Marcus ran inside, and what he saw shocked him. Marcus's father was standing inside the living room looking furious, and Marcus's stepmother was sitting on a chair crying. Marcus was shocked because his father was never at home at that time, and Marcus had never seen his father angry before. Marcus knew that his father was gentle.

'Marcus,' Marcus's father called. Marcus went to his father, and Marcus's father held Marcus and hugged him tightly.

'I'm sorry for all she did to you,' Marcus's father said.

Soon, police officers came, and they took Marcus's stepmother away. Then, a family member of Marcus's stepmother came to take Liam.

'How did you know?' Marcus asked his father.

'Just this afternoon, three people in the neighborhood called me to inform me about her abuse, and a teacher at your school and your proprietor called me too,' Marcus's father said.

Marcus was surprised. Since he had been going through abuse in his stepmother's hands, no one had ever called his father about it. Suddenly, that afternoon, they called. Marcus knew that it was the magic of the wishing well. Marcus was happy as he hugged his father.

Marcus and his father moved from the area, and they lived in a nice neighborhood. Marcus lived happily with his father, and he never suffered abuse again.

Have fun!

About the Author

Olivia Bryce is a versatile author who has explored a wide range of topics in her books, from dinosaurs and mermaids to pirates. She resides in the picturesque countryside of Bozeman, Montana, with her husband Nick. Olivia is an avid reader, actively participating in a Book Club that has thrived for over 20 years. She also enjoys traveling, theater, and has recently discovered the joys of taking long walks through the beautiful Montana landscape. Olivia began writing when her two daughters were babies, and now, thirty years later, she continues to craft engaging stories that captivate readers of all ages.